The Booker and the Post-colonial Indian Award-Winning Novels

The Booker and the Post-colonial Indian Award-Winning Novels

Yakaiah Kathy

GenNext Publication

ISBN : 978-93-8022-309-4

Price : ₹ 690

First Published, 2017

Published by

GenNext Publication
5, Ansari Road
Daryaganj, New Delhi-110002
Phone: 9811692060
E-mail: gennextpublication@hotmail.com

Printed at: G. Print Process, Delhi.

Cataloging in Publication Data—DK
Courtesy: D.K. Agencies (P) Ltd. <docinfo@dkagencies.com>

Kathy, Yakaiah, author.
The Booker and the postcolonial : Indian award-winning novels/Yakaiah Kathy.
pages cm
Includes bibliographical references.
ISBN 9789380223094

1. Indic fiction (English)—History and criticism. 2. Man Booker Prize. 3. Rushdie, Salman. Midnight's children. 4. Roy, Arundhati. God of small things. 5. Desai, Kiran, 1971- Inheritance of loss. 6. Adiga, Aravind. White tiger. I. Title.

PR9484.8.K38 2017 DDC 823.91409954 23

Contents

Acknowledgements

It gives me a great pleasure to express my heartfelt gratitude to my beloved teacher and my role model Professor K. Purushotham who disciplined me in terms of carrying out my research and offering suggestions to go about reading and writing in time and again. I am indebted to him forever.

I profusely thank my teacher Professor M. Rajeshwar who also provides me material time to time to continue my research for many years.

I am also thankful to Professor Pramod K. Nayar, Head, Department of English, University of Hyderabad, for his support for writing a manuscript with his prompt reply through *Whatsup*. I am grateful to him for offering suggestions.

I also thank my beloved wife Kavitha for supporting me time to time to finish my work. Finally, I thank my mother and brothers and sister for their unfailing support.

Yakaiah Kathy

Preface

The book titled "The Booker and The Post-colonial Indian Award Winning Novels" is an attempt to examine the aspect of the representation of India in four novels that have been awarded the Booker Prize. The novels include Salman Rushdie's *Midnight's Children*, Arundhati Roy's *The God of Small Things,* Kiran Desai's *The Inheritance of Loss* and Aravind Adiga's *The White Tiger.* The reason for selecting the Booker Prize winning novels is that the awards and prizes are the quick forms and means of canonisation. The Booker Prize bestows instant credibility on a writer, and ensures assured book sales making it a coveted award for the publishing and bookselling world as well as for the authors. Besides the publication logistics, the Booker Prize also ensures academicisation of the respective work: the awarded novel soon attracts the attention of reviewers, researchers and scholars. Besides forming part of curriculum, the award winning works generate a large body of criticism. Therefore the award winning novels deserve a critical assessment in a full-length study. The criterion for selecting these novels is not merely a matter of category under the Indian Booker Prize novels. The Booker Prize to each of the four novels, in fact, foregrounds four aspects of India that had hither to not been represented in the Indian English novel. The credit for foregrounding the themes of these novels goes to the Booker, without which these novels would have been not what they are. The study, therefore examines the four novels that emerged the new discourses in the criticism.

The study is organised into eight chapters. The first chapter focuses on the existence of the post-colonialism in the Indian fiction in English. This chapter divided into four sections. The first section deals with the emergence of colonial and post-colonialism in the canonical literature. The second section deals with the importance of the Commonwealth Literature prior to the colonial and post-colonial literature. The third section delineates the post-colonialism in the context of Indian fiction in English. The fourth section critiques the significant of post-colonial theorists' who shaped the textual interpretation in an engrossing manner. The second chapter examines the aspect of evolution of the theme of representing India in the Indian English novel. Divided into three sections, the first section of the chapter deals with the origin of the Indian literature and the pre-Independence Indian English novel with a focus on the prominent novelists and their works. The second section examines the concerns of the Indian English novelists in the post-Independence period. The third section traces the role of the criticism in shaping the thrust of the Indian English fiction.

The third chapter, "Canon: The Role of the Booker" explores the controversies that surround the Booker Prize. The literary prizes in general function as the legitimising mechanisms that foreground the symbolic as well as the material effects of the process of literary evaluation. The four Indian novels, which have been selected for the study, have undergone a meticulously evaluated process before being awarded the Booker Prize. The four novels represent a particular aspect of India in each of them. The awarding of the Booker Prize to each of the four novels in turn helped acquire legitimacy at international level. Ever since the beginning of written literature, the privileging of some writers over the other writers has been in place in subtle forms. During the feudal period, writers used to be handpicked by the ruling classes for patronisation. In turn, the writers used their skill for eulogising the rulers. Literary prizes or titles used to be offered by rulers, monarchs and other patrons. They, writes Winegarten, "cannily deployed them for the double purpose of proving their munificence while reconfirming the loyalty of their subjects." The ruler-writer nexus had thus been reciprocal. With the emergence of the capital playing an important role in the promotion of arts and literature, literary awards and prizes took the role of the patronisation of the writers. The patronisation, awards, prizes and other forms of promotion of the authors have been different forms of privileging select writers, which in the present context could be termed the canonisation. This chapter seeks to explore the aspect of the Booker Prize as an important form of canonisation of the novelists both from the former coloniser—England—and the former colonies, against the backdrop of post-colonial literary writing. The second section of the chapter is aimed at problematising the four select novels in the context of the Booker Prizes.

The fourth chapter, "The Personal and the Public: History in *Midnight's Children*" examines the representation of history in the novel. Divided into three sections, the first section of the chapter reviews the criticism on the novel. *Midnight's Children* is undoubtedly one of the most written about novels in the modern period. The novel received both appreciation and criticism, and an attempt has been made to review the criticism for a better understanding of the novel. This section problematises the novel in terms of history. The second section explores the portrayal of Indian history. The thrust of the argument in this section has been that Rushdie contests the official version of history, and provides alternative versions of different historical incidents. The third section of the chapter examines the narrative technique employed in the novel. An attempt has been made to explore such narrative techniques as magic realism, fragmented narration and self-conscious narration.

The fifth chapter, "'Death More Profitable than Life': A Critique of Caste, Patriarchy and Communism in *God of Small Things*" examines *The God of Small Things* in terms of the social institution of caste, reinforced by the religion—be it Hinduism or Syrian Christianity—that treats the untouchables in a subhuman condition. The incident of Velutha's murder testifies that the mechanism of the state and the machinery of police together failed to alleviate the fate of the untouchable predicament of the Dalits. Patriarchy, another important social institution not only marginalises the women, but also reduces them to the condition of objects. Finally, the communist rule in the state of Kerala proved that it failed to mitigate the miserable condition of the Dalits. Arundhati Roy minces no words in being critical of the electoral form of communism, which failed to address caste, one of the seminal institutions that acted as an impediment to the development and modernisation of India as a nation.

The sixth chapter, "'Distant Others': Immigrant Experience in *The Inheritance of Loss*" examines the novel with a focus on the portrayal of the cultural aspect of the urban India. An attempt has been made to map the multicultural aspect vis-à-vis the immigrants. In this respect, *The Inheritance of Loss* occupies an important place in the genre of the recent Indian English novel. Multiculturalism in the context of globalisation has such bearing on the urban populace that the inherent conflict between the native culture and the Western culture is difficult to be resolved, and the genre of the Indian English novel represents this aspect effectively. *The Inheritance of Loss* in this respect is a landmark publication in representing the aspect of multiculturalism.

The seventh chapter, "Representation of Modern India: Social Contexts in *The White Tiger*" examines the novel with a thrust on the social aspect. It has been argued in the chapter that Adiga represents the social contexts of feudal oppression, casteism and dalit suppression. The chapter also examines the individual's growth and the use of the *Bildungsroman* in portraying the subjectivity. The novel has been interpreted with Lisa Lau's concept of 're-Orientalism.' Adiga, as against the Orientalist Western intelligentsia, critiques the socio-economic and political policies of the rulers of modern India, which have failed the aspirations of the people in the Independent country.

The eighth chapter sums up the study by providing the findings of the research. It has been presented, based on the arguments in the preceding chapters, that each of the four Booker Prize winning novels represents an important aspect of India: *Midnight's Children* critiques the rulers of modern India for failing to fulfill the aspirations of the Indians in the post-colonial period; Arundhati Roy's *The God of Small Things* basically critiques the communist rule of Kerala that has proved to be not essentially different from the rightwing political parties; Kiran Desai's *The Inheritance of Loss* presents the impact of multi-culturalism in the context of modern India and Aravind Adiga's *The White Tiger* portrays critically the social contexts of feudal oppression, casteism and dalit suppression.

Chapter - 1

Situating Post-colonialism in Indian Fiction English: A Critique

> His face is turned towards the past.... The angel would like to stay, awaken the dead, and make whole that which has been smashed. But a storm is blowing from Paradise; it has got caught in his wings with such violence that the angel can no longer close them. This storm irrestistibly propels him into the future to which his back is turned, while the pile of debris before him grows skyward. This storm is what we call progress. —*Walter Benjamin*

Post-colonial literature has introduced a new way of thinking to English literature and articulated the colonisers' exploitation of the colonised in various aspects vis-à-vis socio-economic, cultural and political situations across the world. Post-colonialism catapulted in understanding new ideological discourses that assimilated in the colonised nations. It has in fact become the enabling concept, despite the difficulties one can find in defining it. This chapter divided into four sections. The first section deals with the emergence of colonial and post-colonialism in the canonical literature. The second section deals with the importance of the Commonwealth Literature prior to the colonial and post-colonial literature. The third section delineates the post-colonialism in the context of Indian fiction in English. The fourth section critiques the significant of post-colonial theorists' who shaped the textual interpretation in an engrossing manner.

I

Colonialism and imperialism are frequently used in a similar way. The word colonialism according to the *Oxford English Dictionary* (OED), derives from the Roman 'Colonia' which meant 'farm' or 'settlement' and referred to Romans who settled in other lands but still continue their nationality. Accordingly, the OED describes as:

> A settlement in a new country......a body of people who settle in a new locality, forming a community subject to or connected with their parent state; the community so formed, consisting of the original settlers and their descendants and successors, as long as the connection with the parent state is kept up (OED).

The definition precisely jettisons any reference to people other than the colonisers, people who could have started living in the concerned places where British colonies have already been established. Thus, it discards the word colonialism of any aspect of an encounter between peoples, of conquest and domination. It is clearly stated that 'new locality' probably may not be so 'new' and the process of perceiving a community might be very unacceptable. Colonialism was not a uniform process in various parts of the world but everywhere it controlled the native inhabitants and the foreigners into the most complex and traumatic relationship in human history. In Shakespeare's *The Tempest,* 'his single major addition to the story he found in certain pamphlets about a shipwreck in the Bermudas was to make the island inhabited before Prospero's arrival' (Hulme 69).

That single addition turned the romance into an allegory of the colonial encounter. The process of establishing a community in the colonised country apparently denotes un-forming or reforming the communities that prevailed there already and introduced a greater amount of practices such as trade, unfair discussions, conflict, indiscriminate killing, subjugation and rebellions. Those practices entailed and have been altered by a different writings –public and private records, letters, trade documents, government papers, fiction and scientific literature. Further, these practices and writings are what contemporary studies of colonialism and post-colonialism that would make sensible.

The prominent literary critic Ania Loomba adds that "colonialism can be defined as the conquest and control of other people's land and goods. But colonialism accordingly is no longer merely the expansion of different Europeans powers into Asia, Africa or the Americas from the sixteenth century onwards" (Loomba, 8). There has been a recurrent and pervasive feature of human history. She further offers a clear description of the colonialism.

> At its height in the second century AD, the Roman Empire stretched from Armenia to Atlantic. Under Genghis Khan in the thirteenth century, the Mongols conquered the Middle East as well as China. The Aztec empire was established when, from the fourteenth to the sixteenth centuries, one of the various ethnic groups who settled in the valley of Mexico subjugated the others. Aztecs extracted tributes in services and goods from conquered regions, as did the Inca Empire which was the largest pre-industrial state in the Americas. In the fifteenth century too, various kingdoms in southern India came under the control of the Vijayanagar Empire.............At the beginning of the eighteenth century, it still extended from the Mediterranean to the Indian Ocean, and the Chinese empire was larger than anything Europe had seen (Loomba 8).

Contemporary European colonialism however cannot be prevented from these previous histories of association with the Crusades or the Moorish invasion of Spain, the heroic exploits of Mongol rulers or the legendary wealth of the Incas or the Mughals were real or imagined fuel for the European journey to different parts of the world. And yet, these newer European travels ushered in new and various types of colonial communities which changed the entire world in a way that these other colonialism did not.

Many questions were cropped up of the Europeans and Westerners' establishment in the colonised countries. All of these descriptions have in fact been offered to account for the global power and drastic effects of European colonialisms. "Marxists critical thinking on the subject situates a significant distinction between the two: while previous colonialisms were pre-capitalist, modern colonialism was established alongside in Western Europe" (Bottmore 81).

However, the contemporary colonialism contributed more than extract tribute, goods and wealth from the countries that conquered. Nevertheless, it restructured the discipline of the economies of the latter, driving them into a patch of relationships with their own, subsequently there was a flow of human and natural resources between colonised and colonial countries. This flow prevailed in both directions- slaves and indentured labour as well as raw materials that have been transported to change goods in the metropolis or in other places for metropolitan usage but the colonies also provided noticeable remarks for European goods. As a result, slaves used to be shifted from Africa to the America. In the West Indian plantations, they produced sugar utility in Europe, and the same raw cotton was shifted from India in turn those who have own production cloth adversely suffered. In whatever direction, human beings and goods travelled, the benefits always were given to their native country.

One of the most primacy dimensions of English literatures today is the projection of post-colonial literatures, those literatures written in English in formerly colonised societies. This study offered a good amount of theoretical ideas, concepts, problems and debates, and these have been observed in a wide range of articles, essays, lectures and books published or written from every parts of the world.

In the beginning of the twentieth century, the British Empires have occupied major parts of the world like Africa, Asia, Australia, Canada, the Caribbean and Ireland. At the beginning of the twenty-first century, the British colonies have slowly fizzled out from the native countries. The phrase 'the British Empire' is probably usually used these days in the past tense, suggesting a historical period and different patch of relationships which are no longer existed. In short, the twentieth century has been treated as the ending of legacy of colonials, and the adverse austerity for millions of people who were involved in the authority of the British crown. However, the English has continued its colonial power in the Caribbean and South Atlantic during the twenty-first century period. In addition, the leftovers and inventive legacies of both colonialism and decolonisation remain fundamentally considerable formative elements in a variety of contemporary disciplines, such as anthropology, economics, art, global politics, international capitalism, and the mass-media.

Colonialism has influenced in different forms and has caused different effects around the world, but one can feel as precise as one can define its meaning. It is argued by considering its relationship with two other terms: Capitalism and Imperialism. As Denis Judd argues that "no one can doubt that the desire for profitable trade, plunder and enrichment was the primary force that led to the establishment of the Imperial structure" (Judd, 3). Judd asserts that colonialism was established in terms of the business interest of the Western nations that developed from the late seventeenth and early eighteenth centuries. The native lands are grabbed for establishing the administration and settlement. Their primordial object is to instill a motivation in terms of establishment of their own business in abroad and for improving the Western goods as well as obtaining the natural resources and labour, controlling the different lands and peoples at the cheaper level. Colonialism was a profit making commercial element, gaining wealth and riches to Western nations through the financial benefits, reward and riches. Hence, colonialism and capitalism share equally supportive relationship with each other.

'Colonialism' is recurrently substituted with 'imperialism', but in truth the terms mean different things. As Peter Childs and Patric Williams argue:

> Imperialism is an ideological concept which upholds the legitimacy of the economic and military control of one nation by another. Colonialism, however, is only one form of practice which results from the ideology of imperialism, and specifically concerns the settlement of one group of people in a new location. Imperialism is not strictly concerned with the issue of settlement; it does not demand the settlement of different places in order to work. They define imperialism as 'the extension and expansion of trade and commerce under the protection of political, legal and military control' (Williams 227).

It is observed that how imperialism does not need the settlement of different section of people from the imperial nation in another location. In the following terms, colonialism is one but it is not the only way of colonialism is almost over today. In fact, the *Imperialism* goes about promptly in securing wealth and power through the perpetual economic exploitation of other nations, as Western nations such as America are still involved in imperial acts. Thus, as Benita Parry puts it, "colonialism is a specific and mutable states, one which preceded the rule of international finance capitalism and whose formal ending imperialism has survived" (Parry 34).

Colonialism is a representation of historical manifestation of imperialism pertaining to certain places and times. In the same way, one can observe the British Empire as one form of an imperial economic and political template. Thus, one can endorse Elleke Boemer's judicious definition of colonialism as the settlement of territory, the exploration or development of resources, and the attempt to govern the indigenous inhabitants of occupied lands. Note in this definition (a) the emphasis on the settlement of land (b) the economic relationship at the heart of colonialism, and (c) the unequal relations of power which colonialism constructs" (Boehmer 2).

Boehmer's phrase 'the attempt to govern' looks at the ways in which British colonialism is no longer successful all the time in achieving its aims, and received with the acts of resistance since beginning by aboriginal populace of colonised lands as well as members of European communities who established their rule across the world. It does not show interest to delay power and authority to the imperial 'motherland'. Concerning the imperial project of the British Empire, there are three prominent periods of *Decolonisation* when the colonised nations obtained the right to govern their affairs. The first period is to announce the American independence during the eighteenth century. The second period covers the end of the nineteenth century to the first decade of the twentieth century. It concerns the creation of the 'dominions' this was the term applied to describe the nations of Canada, Australia, New Zealand and South Africa. These nations assimilates in larger European populations that settled in overseas and often violently displacing or destroying the different community peoples of these lands-Native Indians in Canada, Aboriginal communities in Australia and New Zealand, black African peoples in South Africa.

There were of course many countries. One basic cause was due in different means to the growth of various nationalist movements both in the 'Coloniser' and 'Colonised' colonies that increase subject to British colonial dominion. In addition, the aftermath of Second World War particularly, Britains' position as a world economic power that has declined adversely, whereas America and the Soviet Union have become strong in terms of military powers of the post-war era. The British Empire has become the most expensive to administer and it made economic sense to give away its administration of colonial affairs to its people, however, the colonised peoples were prepared for the displacement of power. Writing of the disparate projects that seek to establish alternative protocols in disciplinary studies, Edward Said finds their common feature to be that all work out of a secular, marginal and oppositional consciousness, posit 'noting less than new objects of knowledge..... new theoretical models that upset or at the very least radically alter the prevailing paradigmatic norms and are political and practical in as much as they intend....the end of dominating 'coercive systems of knowledge" (Said 234).

The mark of colonial aftermath is triggered by the range of ambivalent cultural moods and developments which go together with periods of transition and translation. It is in the fact that a true moment of arrival of celebration with the rhetoric of independence and the artistic ecstasy of self-invention. This is the spirit with Saleem Sinai, the hero of Salman Rushdie's *Midnight's Children*, primarily delivers an account of the mythical sense of personification that connects to the coincidence of his birth and the new Indian nation on the stroke of the midnight hour on 15 August 1947: 'for the next three decades, there was to be no escape. Soothsayers had prophesied me, newspapers celebrated my arrival, politicos ratified my authenticity' (Rushdie, 9). Probably, as Rushdie's Indian everyman, Saleem Sinai subsequently identifies the colonial aftermath, is also filled with the anxieties and fears of failure that necessarily attempt to satisfy the historical burden of expectation. In Sinai's words 'I must work fast, faster than Scheherazade, if I am to end up meaning-yes, meaning-something. I admit it: above all things, I fear absurdity, (Rushdie, 9). Largely, Saleem presumed that the inheritors of the colonial aftermath might represent a new world completely. Sinai's fell into independent India by the crippling optimism of Nehru's historical narration of post-coloniality, 'a moment comes, which comes but rarely in history, when we step out from the old to the new, when age ends, and when the soul of a nation long suppressed finds utterance...' (Rushdie, 116).

Although it is out of context to crop up the idea of Frederic Jameson's observation on post-modernism that the celebratory of cyborg post-coloniality is ceased by "something like an imperative to grow new organs, to expand our object and our body to same new, yet unimaginable, perhaps impossible, dimensions" (Jameson, 39). However, in following this significance, post-coloniality is utterly forced to discuss the disagreements emerging from its genuine historical existence, its post-coloniality, or political and chronological derivation from colonialism and its cultural obligation should be initiated in a sensible way. Thus, its main aim of arrival into independence is based on its capacity to expect and perform an imperative departure from the colonial past.

Albert Memmi, the Tunisian anti-colonial movement and intellectual, critically argued that the colonial aftermath basically came out to be traitor in its hope that the construction of a new world would automatically arising from the physical damage of colonialism. Memmi observes that the successful subjects of its aftermath necessarily demean the psychological domination of colonial past on the post-coloniality. In his words: 'the day oppression ceases, the new man is supposed to emerge before our eyes immediately. Now, I do not like to say so, but I must, since decolonisation has demonstrated it: this is not the way it happened. The colonised lives for a long time before we see that really new man (Memmi 88).

Memmi's political resistance offers description of post-coloniality as a historical imperative by noticeable structure of liberation and the hidden perseverance of unfreedom. He suggests that the customary of the post-colonial territorial between reaching and departure, liberation and dependence, its foundation in the outstanding initiation and memories of subordination. 'The perverse longevity of the colonised is nourished, in part, by persist colonial hierarchies of knowledge and value which reinforce what Edward Said calls the 'dreadful secondariness of different cultural peoples'(Said 207). Hence, the national independence is coated with the superficial veneer barely disguises the foundational economic, cultural and political damage induced by colonial occupation. As Said argues 'Colonisation is a fate with lasting, indeed grotesquely unfair results' (Said 207).

The contradictions of national liberation according to writers like Memmi and Said insist that post-colonialism did not allow the decline of colonialism. Despite the fact that its dissatisfaction tone, this verdict is probably framed by the benign intention to ameliorate from the post-colonial fiction of radical segregation from Europe. The prefix 'post', as Lyotard has written, elaborates the conviction 'that it is both possible and necessary to break with tradition and institute absolutely new ways of living and thinking (Lyotard 90). This type of successful strong conviction changes its manifestation of the future out of the calmness and omissions of historical amnesia. It is understood by a false conviction in the irrelevalent and requisite of the past. In Lyotard's judgment, 'this rupture is in fact a way of forgetting or repressing the past, that is to say, repeating it and not surprising it' (Lyotard 90). It might conclude by stating that the dream of post-colonialism is paralysed finally in contagious to the unthinkable and undecided past. The period of recovery is needlessly extended on account of its denial to recap and identify its existence with the harmful malaise of colonisation.

If post-coloniality is viewed as a situation that is triggered by the repercussions of a self-determined historical amnesia, then the theoretical imperative of post-colonialism exists, partly, in its faculty to expand the forgotten memories of condition. Further, the colonial aftermath for betterment of life and therapeutic theory that is resulted in making the task of recalling and retrieving the colonial history. This kind of work may be differentiated with what Lyotard explains as the psychoanalytic method of *anamnesis,* or analysis-that impulses patients 'to elaborate their current problems by freely associating apparently inconsequential details with past situations-allowing them to uncover hidden meanings in their lives and their behaviour' (Lyotard 93). In following this implication, post-colonial theory necessarily commits *per se* to a comprehensive work of historical and psychological 'recovery'. If scholars would carefully research in terms of digging out the historical details, it has relatively forcing political obligation to assist the different disciplines of post-coloniality to comfort with the gaps and fissures of their condition, and thereby learn to go on with self-understanding.

In the context of post-colonial limbo, Salman Rushdie throws a light on a wonderful moment of traitor and reconciliation in *Midnight's Children*, when the main character and narrator, Saleem Sinai tells the cultural assimilation and comic misrecognition of his celebrated birth. In the beginning of the novel, Amina Sinai finds a great difficulty to give birth to a child in Dr Narlinkar's Nursing Home, impoverished woman named Vanita experiences neglected labour in the 'charity ward'. She is about to give birth to a child, is a result of illicit relationship with an Englishman, William Methwold, who speaks high of his background especially imperialistic East India Company officer. After the children were delivered, a proactive midwife Mary Pereira swaps Amina's and Vanita's babies around. Thus, Saleem Sinai, eulogised by Nehru himself as the child of independent India, is unwillingly the son of departing coloniser. But this event, as the adult Saleem emphases, is the allegorical condition of all those who followed the colonial aftermath: 'In fact all over the new India, the dream we all shared, children were being born who were only partially the offspring of their parents' (Rushdie 118). In his self conscious- narration, Saleem Sinai at the same time defies the guilt of unathenticity and the willingness to refuse the knowledge of his faulty genealogy. The Sinais finally reunite themselves to the fact of Methwold's survival of legitimate to the amalgamate inadequacies of their own post-coloniality. As Saleem explains: 'When we eventually discovered the crime of Mary Pereira, we all found that it made that it made no difference! I was still their son; they remained my parents. In a kind of collective failure of imagination, we learned that we simply could not think our way out of our pasts…' (Rushdie118). This might change this narrative wisdom slightly to say that maybe the only is by contemplating thoroughly about the pasts.

II

This section delineates the emergence of the commonwealth literature that totally marked a difference in terms of form and concept in publishing the texts. The most significant dimension for post colonialism was the growth of the study of Commonwealth literature. Literary critics began to use the term Commonwealth literature from the 1950s to explain literatures in English emerged from a selection of countries with a history of colonialism. It incorporated the writers from colonial and colonised community writers belonging to the concerned countries which were in the process of gaining independence from British colonials such as the African, Caribbean and South Asian nations.

Literary critics began to differentiate a fast growing body of literature written in English that included work by stalwarts as R. K. Narayan, George Lamming, Katherine Mansfield and Chinua Achebe. The term 'Commonwealth Literature' deals with a particular area of study an attempt to explore and identify the importance of literary development and how it has got its own importance in the field of world literature. Significantly, both American and Irish Literature were not incorporated in early formulation of the field. Commonwealth literatures, then, was associated exclusively with selected countries with a history of colonialism.

There is a shift from 'colonial' to 'Commonwealth' probably endorses a specific version of history in which the position of colonised countries gladly alters from submissive to equality. However, one can discard agreeing this selective view, no longer least because the economic and political relations between Britain and Commonwealth nations have differed from equal. The recognition and study of 'Commonwealth Literature' undoubtedly reverberated the tenor of the usage of 'Commonwealth' but it also has its own problems. In other words, the term offered a shared, remarkable literary legacy between different and variable nations. It obviously projected unity in diversity- revealingly, the plural term 'Commonwealth literatures' was sparingly applied. As A Norman Jeffares declared in 1964, "addressing the first conference of Commonwealth literature at the University of Leeds in England, one reads because they bring new ideas, new interpretations of life to us" (Jeffares 14). It is not clear whether the 'us' in this sentence referred to the diverse audience at the conference comprising writers and academics from many Commonwealth nations, or specifically British readers in particular. 'Commonwealth Literature' may well have been created in an attempt to bring together writings from around the world on an equal footing, yet the assumption remained that these texts were addressed primarily to a western English speaking readership. The 'Commonwealth literature' was never fully free from the older and it has become more imperious connotations of the term. The Western theorists belong to the commonwealth literature has a patches of relationship between the literature and the nation. In the introduction to a collection of essays A. Mcleod proposed that

> The genesis of a local literature in the commonwealth countries has almost always been contemporaneous with the development of a truly nationalist sentiment: the larger British colonies such as Fiji, Hong Kong and Malta, where there are relatively large English speaking populations, have produced not literature, even in the broadcast sense of the term. The reason probably lies in the fact that they have, as yet, no sense of national identity, no cause to follow, no common goal (Mcleod 8).

Numerous critics noted that the new ideas and new interpretations of life in commonwealth literature in national and cultural recognition. This was definitely one of the functions of the texts regarded as 'commonwealth literature' and its nationalist representations.

Despite the fact that drawing the attention of the alleged nationalist purposes of much commonwealth literature often occupied second fiddle to more abstract concerns that ignored from the national context. The critics were preoccupied with an identifying a common set of concerns of commonwealth literature whether produced in India, Australia or the Caribbean. It is alleged that reaching across national borders and dealing with universal concerns. Common-wealth literature possibly concerned with the national and cultural aspects but the best writing has become unfamiliar to transcend them too.

Exploring the editorial to be the foremost edition of the *Journal of Commonwealth Literature* published in September 1965. The editorial team observed that there is a need to identify the important cultural differences between writers from different locations. But it also revealed that the ways in which literature from commonwealth nations was integrated through the types of commonwealth literature:

> The name of the journal is simply a piece of convenient shorthand, which should no account be construed as a perverse underwriting of any concept of a single, culturally homogenous body of writings to be thought of as 'Commonwealth Literature'... Clearly, all writing...takes its place within the body of English literature, and becomes subject to the criteria of excellence by which literary works in English are judged, but the pressures that act upon a Canadian writing in English differ significantly from those operating upon an Indian using a language not his mother tongue, just as both kinds from those that affect an Englishman (Journal of Commonwealth literature 1).

Every responsible writer undergoes pressures historically and culturally that differed across time and space. According to the editorial team, the texts have been studied as commonwealth literature were written apparently in English, they were to be analysed in relation to English literature with the similar objective applied to describe the literary value of the age old English classics. It was obviously comparable with the English literary canon that executed as the means of measuring its significance. As A. Norman Jeffares put it:

> a Commonwealth writer of value 'wants ultimately to be judged not because he gives us a picture of life in a particular place, in a particular situation, but by the universal, lasting quality of his writings, judged by neither local nor yet national standards. Good writing is something which transcends borders, whether local or national, whether of the mind or of the spirit' (Jeffares vxiii).

Commonwealth literature was a small group of canonical literature, being evaluated in terms of derived from the traditional study of English that emphasised the values of existing and universality. As Walsh discusses a novel by George Lamming. Lamming hails from Barbados in the Caribbean and has African ancestry. This is what Walsh made of Lamming's novel *Season of Adventure* (1960)

> In this novel the African theme and connection become stronger and more positive, although it is never allowed to puff into a

merely abstract existence. Indeed, Lamming's achievement is to make us hear the stream of the humiliated and persecuted and to make it simultaneously a metaphor for the damage *universal in mankind* (Walsh 53).

Walsh recognises African elements in the novel that bear witness to the context of Lamming's role as a writer. But Africa is merely a 'theme' and not allowed to be the *Primary* focus of the work that is the novel's attention to the damage universal in mankind. Later in his book Walsh reads the Australian Patric White's novel *Voss* (1957) in similar terms, as 'powerful and humane work coloured with the light and soaked with the sweat and personality of Australia, (White 134). Hence, for critics like Walsh, commonwealth literature basically focuses on the similar pre-occupations with the human condition as did Jane Austin or George Eliot. National disparities certainly significant, stating the newness of 'personality', 'light' and 'colour' but finally these national particulars were secondary to the basic worldwide meaning of the work.

Presently, this type of critical approach that makes secondary the historical contexts that state a work of literature is often described as 'liberal humanist'. For liberal humanists, the most of the 'literary texts presumably transcend the provincial contexts of their early production that deal with the human development of all times and places. As far as self-introspection is concerned; critics of commonwealth literature seem to be very much like liberal humanists. The so called critics had no idea that how texts were read so impressively might resist their reading components and understand the assumptions of universality and timelessness that canonised the criteria of 'good writing'. In fact, one of the fundamental differences that post-colonial critics have emerged from their commonwealth contemporaries is their insistence that historical, geographical and cultural specifics are very important to both the writing and reading of a text. It cannot be conspicuously bracketed as secondary element or background, conformed to a critical status quo. Those texts were considered particularly neither important nor resistance to challenge the western criteria of excellence used to read them effectively.

The critical approach of the text is mainly focused on the ease and felicity made them exciting to read and supported to describe the nation. But the prime differences were repressed by the identification of universal themes within the texts that have hidden aesthetic criteria of the west. The *various* preoccupations and contexts of texts have apparently become very significant than alleged *similar* abstract qualities for post-colonial critics. However, it would be an unfair to disapprove the text of previous generations of critics of commonwealth literature in the pretext of present context. Obviously critics like Jeffares and Walsh belong to a previous phase of literary criticism that was immediately challenged in the former decades of the century. But they and others played instrumental role in acquiring Commonwealth literature as a prominent group of artistic endeavour and as a comfortable area of academic study.

As Shirley Chew has explained, 'a paradox sits at the heart of the commonwealth: described as a free association of equal and mutually cooperating nations, it is nevertheless drawn together by a shared history of colonial exploitation, dependence and interchange (Shirley Chew 32). When the study of commonwealth literature was traced in the philanthropic spirit of this paradox, the critical approach of post-colonialism was to focus on the darker side of world. During the 1970s and 1980s, many critics attempted to discard the liberal humanist bias conceived in commonwealth literature in understanding the literature in new ways.

III

Indian writing in English has presented the demeaning artistic response suggested by the allegations of westernisation is probably missing from these writers' work. Rushdie promulgates excessive objects of Indian style of writing. In general, it is a short enduring virus and those whom it influences soon fabricate and find their true voices.

Paradoxically, during the pre-independence, India has many vernacular language writers who could present worthy books; Bankim Chandra Chatterjee, Rabindranath Tagore, Dr Muhammad Iqbal, Mirza Ghalib, Bibhuti Bhushan Banerjee and Premchand, the prominent

Hindi writer of, among many others, the popular novel of rural life, *Godaan*, or *The Gift of a Cow*. The writers who intend to look for their leading legendaries, for example, O.V V. Vijayan (Malayalam), Suryakant Tirupathi Nirala (Hindi), Nirmala Verma (Hindi), U. R. Anthamurthy (Kannada), Suresh Joshi (Gujarati), Amrita Pritam (Punjabi), Qurratulain Haider (Urdu), or Ismat Chughati (Urdu), and contributed their intellectual capital effectively.

The debut Indian novel in English a dud, *Rajmohan's Wife* (1864) is an underprivileged melodramatic aspect. The author Bankim, distinguished to Bengali and immediately gained great reputation. For seventy years or so, there had been no English language fiction of any quality. It was the period of independence, 'Midnight's parents', one might call them who are the true embodiment of this new tradition. Of these, Mulk Raj Anand had imitated the genre of both James Joyce and Marx but most of all, maybe by the teachings of Mahatma Gandhi. Raja Rao, a renowned scholar of Sanskrit, wrote passionately of the need to project an Indian English for himself but even his much-acclaimed juxtaposes of village life, *Kanthapura*, it presents at once complex and archaic expression. The autobiographer Nirad C. Choudari is a promising scholar to discuss contrary aspects. He argues that "India has no culture of its own, and that whatever we now call Indian culture was brought in from outside by the successive waves of conquerors." This climate of opinion was not impressed with his fellow Indians and he prevented *The Autobiography of an Unknown Indiani* from getting the popularity as the masterpiece.

Another prominent writers of the first generation, R. K. Narayan and G.V. Desani, have had ambivalent careers. Narayan has many books to his credit, while Desani is the author of a single work of fiction, *All About H Hatter*, and that singleton volume is already fifty years old. Desani is not known, whereas Narayan became world popular writer for a creation of the fiction world "Malgudi". It has become very exciting place for the readers. Much of Narayan will be discussed in the forthcoming chapter.

G.V. Desani has fallen so far from favour that the magnificent text *All About Hatter* is presently out of print everywhere. Milan Kundra once said that " all modern literature descends from either

Richardson's *Clarrissa* or Sterne's *Tristram Shandy*, and if Narayan's is India's Richardson then Desani is his Shandean other." Hatters's idazzling, puzzling, leaping prose is the first genuine effort to go beyond the Englishness of the English language.

The elegant of Nayantara Sahgal's memoir *Parison and Chocolate Cake* is parralled by the liveliness and grace of her fiction, while Kamal Markandaya's *Nector in a Sieve* is a portrayal of village life. Ved Mehta represented in *Vedi*, is an autobiographical element, delineates the reminiscences of childhood blindness that is an account of cruelties and kindness with equal affect. Ruthprawar Jhabvala has published short stories substantially. As an author, she is sometimes demeaned in India because the description of rootless intellectual in their regional identities. She is the popularly known for the award winning screen writer.

Anita Desai is one of the premier Indian living writers. Her novel *In Custody* perhaps is one of the best novels to her credit. She uses English to depict the decadence of another language like Urdu which has the highest cultural validity. One of the most important figures in the story of modern literature, V.S. Naipaul, ignorantly away from Indian canonical writing. His three non-fiction books on India, *An area of Darkness*, *A Wounded Civilisation* and *India*. Many critics have surprised with the harshness of his responses. His writings belong to partly the Indian culture and partly of the Trinidadian culture. His prominent works are based on the cosmopolitanism and multiculturalism concepts.

In *An Area of Darkness,* Naipaul's comments on Indian writers elicit in this reader a characteristic mixture of agreement and dissent. When he writes,

> the feeling is widespread that, whatever English might have done for Tolstoy, it can never do justice to the Indian language writers. This is possible, what I read of them in translation did not encourage me to read more. Premchand....Turned out to be a minor fabulist...Other writers quickly fatigued me with their assertion that poverty was sad, that death was sad... many of the 'modern' short stories were only refurbished folk tales...(Quoted in Rushdie's introduction xx).

Then he probably explores not in a frightful way, when he continues to say, “The novel discusses the western concern towards the Indians with the condition of men, a response to the here and now” (Rushdie xx). Radhakrishnan is an erstwhile President of India said that ‘the basic human hunger for the ‘unseen’. It is not a good qualification for the writing and reading of novels. It is true that many educated elite go in for a deeply incomprehensible form of critic-mysticism.

During the period of 1980s and 1990s, the emergence of quality of writing has achieved its own ease and felicity. Bapsi Sindhwa is technically Pakistani, but this anthology has necessarily not about the partitions. His famous novel *Ice Candy Man* derived here, is one of the best responses to the agony of the segregation of the subcontinent. Gita Hariharan, less known writer than Sindhwa and Mehta, confirm the quality of contemporaneous writing on Indian women.

Over a period of time, the different genres of writing have evolved in the Indian fiction in English. The Stendhalian realism of a writer like Rohinton Mistry, the equally authenticity but easier, more appealing prose of Vikram Seth and the impressive social observation of Upamanyu Chatterjee is against the more different manner of Vikram Chandra and the touches of amazing style in Mukul Kesavan. Amitav Ghosh’s prominent work *In an Antique Land*, is the best known for the non-fiction study of Indian and Egypt. Sara Suleri, whose memoir *Meatless Days* is, like Bapsi Sidhwa’s *Ice Candy Man,* a traveller from across the Pakistani polarised town, is a non-fiction writer of extreme naturalist and generous. And Amit Chaudari’s poesy, unique style, wonderful prose is impressively impossible to place in any category at all.

Most interestingly, another talented writer has emerged in the same generation Keralian writer Arundhati Roy has arrived with a magnificent style of writing that paved the way to acquire the world recognition with the publication of *The God of Small Things.* There are the equally the other debuts of two first novelists. Ardashir Vakil’s *Beach Boy* and Kiran Desai’s S*trange Happenings in the Guava Orchard* have distinctive style of narration of India by the original style. The Vakil’s book is energetic, funny and fast, Kiran Desai, luxurious and ecstatically imagined. Kiran Desai is the daughter of Anita, she establishes the legacy of modern Indian Fiction English. However, she is very much possessive about her own author, the articulations of new themes, and challenging with the English language is far removed from proving abortive and continues to give birth to new children obsessed with different things. However, on the map of world literature, India has been undersized for too long, the writers who are ensuring that sixty nine years of independence India has got its own identity in terms of the quality of writing in various fields in the world.

However, Post-colonial Indian writing in English, however seized upon an idea that changes in social, political, economic and cultural realms that ultimately attributed a marked variety to Indian fiction. New tendency such as blending realism and fantasy and integrate Indian and Western narrative forms have also prevailed on.

Salman Rushdie, Vikram Seth, Arundhati Roy and Shashi Tharoor, through their primitive modes of story-telling, constructed India and 'Indianness' in their works. Bama's *Sangati* and Sivakami's *The Grip of Change* have critiqued a harrowing experience of dalit women in caste ridden post-colonial Indian from feminist perspective. Indian-English writers today show India from the transnational point.

The prison and exile writings of Indian immigrants made way for the Diaspora Indian English writers who live in the suburbs of the developed nations but, like their predecessors, draw upon the Indian subcontinent for their writings. Writers like V.S. Naipaul, Anita Desai, Kiran Desai, Bharati Mukherjee, Vikram Seth, Rohinton Mistry, Jumpha Lahari and Hari Kunzru, Aravind Adiga, Jeet Tayal, Anuradha Roy explored the problems faced by the displaced people in their adopted homes, contested the binary division of the East and the West and also questioned the traditional understanding of concepts like 'home', 'nation', 'insider' and 'outsider'. Translation of regional Indian literature, by depicting the regional diversity and multiplicity of the Indian subcontinent, has brought out the quality of Indian literature in the global literary scenario.

The world draws the attention of suppressed voices of the marginalised and tribal people in the works of Mahaswetha Devi,

Indira Goswami and Gopinath Mohanthy through translations. Post-colonial writing generated interesting themes like Partition novel, Diasporic writing, Indian women's writing, Historical, mythological narrative of Raj, Indian literature in English translation and literature of the other.

Post-colonial Indian writing in English has witnessed a great change in terms of theme and form. Writers like Raja Rao, Salman Rushdie and Amitav Ghosh and Arundhati Roy, Vikram Seth, Jumpha Lahari adopted the native idiom of the English language so as to represent contemporaneous issues of the post-independence history. Writers belong to this period probably picked up the problems of post-independence India where the people have been plagued by the poverty stricken society. They restructure the Indian situations vis-à-vis socio-political, cultural and political condition of the country. C.D. Narsimahiah points out that:

> I have no time for such theoretical, because futile and fatuous, questions as: Can Indians write in English? My position is simply this: here before us is a concrete situation. Which is that Indians have for over a century and half used English in speech and writing with such conspicuous ability and that as scholars we should try and understand the nature of that achievement, and if the term achievement irritates some. I shall say, effort (Narsimahiah 4).

Many critics have disagreed with C.D. Narsimahiah's ideas on Indian English Literature (IEL), is no longer need a requisite for those who float the idea of liberty to reinstitute the Indian English debate. So far as the critical understanding of it is concerned, it generates an interesting discussion on Narsimahiah whose view is a futile and fatuous question, whereas admitting the principle with what he generates by offering an answer. In other words, a large number of questions have been posed on the quality of writing in English in Indian English literature. He is neither supportive of roots nor shoots of the Indian writing in English. His strong conviction towards the writing of Indian literature remains same. Over a period of time, the writers have marketed themselves abroad by exploring the interesting themes in the field of Indian writing in English in representing the Indian Diasporas.

IV

This section deals with the post-colonial theory that has altered the new way of studying literature in terms of all aspects. The prominent writers like Edward Said, Homi K. Bhabha, Gayatri Spivak's works hobnobbed with the idea of reading the literary text. Post-colonial theory offers philosophical underpinnings that paved the way in understanding historical genealogy of the text as well as the author. There are numerous post-colonial theorists figured in the twentieth century literature, tremendously influenced in critiquing the author and text and reader. This is in fact an idea introduced by French philosopher Jackques Derrida who shaped the concept of understanding the text in a same vein. His primordial idea of 'deconstruction' brought out remarkable change in analysing the text in a more fruitful way. However, his textual ideology has greatly influenced in the realm of literary text. Ever since the idea of Derrida deconstruction "metaphysics of presence' is cropped up, the canonical literature has witnessed a great paradigm shift in representing the work of art in the world. Among many post-colonial theorists, only the holy trinity of post-colonial theorists' ideology is explored in the section: Edward Said, Homi K. Bhabha, and Gayatri Chakravarthi Spivak.

With the publication of Edward Said's *Orientalism,* the reading of post-colonial theory witnessed a memory of subordination in westerns' negative representation of the eastern in the print and media. In response to the negative portrayal of eastern by western, Said critically attacked on the western media by publishing *Orientalism* (1978). Said sees Orientalism as a discourse by which European culture was able to manage and even produce the orient politically, sociologically, militarily, ideologically, scientifically and imaginatively during the post-enlightenment period, he stated:

> Taking the eighteenth century as a very roughly defined starting point, Orientalism can be defined as the corporate institution for dealing with the Orient- dealing with it by making statements

> about it, describing it, by teaching it, settling it, ruling over it, in short Orientalism as a western style for dominating, restructuring and having authority over the orient (Said 21).

It is shown explicitly that the concept of orientalism has been negatively portrayed that how the western controlled by negating the orient's own voice. He says of Flaubert's Egyptian courtesan that "she never spoke of herself, she never represented her emotions, presence, or history. He spoke for and represented" (Said 6). She was in silence because of the evaluation of different cultures of Europeans, "Orientals were rarely seen or looked at; they were seen through, analysed not as citizens, or even people, but as problems to be solved or confined" (Said 207), as "silent shadows to be animated by the orientalist" (Said 208). "The orient" was a consistent, static entity of study. Within a quotation by Gertrude Bell, Said identifies rejection with the use of "the Arab" "such as to wipe out any traces of individual Arabs with narratable life historicalries" (Said 229). In other words, Said critiques that what was lacking in contemporary western culture was "the orient as a genuinely felt and experienced force (Said 208).

In contradiction of the static view of the orient, Said acknowledges the need for the narrative: "narrative asserts the power of men to be born, develop, and die, the tendency of institutions and actualities to change" (Said 240). Said recognises the complex dynamic of human life "as what he calls "historically as narrative" (Said 247). Describing of literature, Said says:

> One of the striking aspects of the new American social science attention to the orient is its singular avoidance of literature.[…] what seem [sic] to matter far more to the regional expert are 'facts', of which a literary text is perhaps a disturber. The net effect of this reduced to "attitudes", "trends", statistics; in short, dehumanised. Since an Arab poet or novelist [..] writes of his experiences of his values, of his humanity [..], he effectively disrupts the various patterns […] by which the orient is represented. A literary text speaks more or less directly of a living reality (Said 291).

Said concludes about the orientalism by saying "orientalism failed to identify with human experience, failed also to see it as human experience" (Said 328) and that he likes to notice a challenge to the worldwide hegemony of orientalism with his work of art as a great contribution to this challenge.

Gayatri Chakravarthi Spivak's view as 'Subaltern'. Spivak is a prolific contemporary deconstructionist who explored the issues of gender and race. Her use of the term 'subaltern' is influenced by the Italian philosopher Antonio Gramsci who voiced it for the subordinate position in terms of class, gender, race and culture. Spivak's much acclaimed essay 'Can the Subaltern Speak?-advocates the way the 'subaltern' woman is constructed, as absent or silent or not listened to.

The subordination of women in post-colonial point of view is the main issue that her work confronts. The principal argument of the essay is that the contradiction between patriarchy and imperialism, subjective nations and objective construction of the eastern by the western and the figure of woman disappears from the main stream of society and a marginal position of tradition and modernisation.

Spivak uses the term 'Subaltern' for women, blacks, the colonised and proletarians. Subalternity comes to denote the oppressive dominance of coloniser thinking and an allegory of the displacement of the gendered and colonised subject by the imposition of narratives of internationalism and nationalism. The way, violence is erupted in a form of thought upon the east is of great concern to Spivak. She presents 'the third world' to be a creation of the west that ceases non-western cultures into an imperial representation. Spivak's representation of 'Worlding' that creates 'colonised space' is existed into the world and it is obliged to evoke as a part of a world necessarily constituted by Europeanism.

In the processing of different kinds of formulations, one of the pitfalls is attributing a complete power to the hegemonic discourse in making the native and not providing enough space for the opposing of the native. That brings us to Bhabha, the third prominent figure of the holy trinity and his key objective is 'mimicry'.

'Mimicry' juxtaposes a gap between the norm of civility as presented by European enlightenment and changed the colonial imitation. It functions as the secret weapon of anti-colonial behaviour and is an ambivalent combination of deference and disobedience. Bhabha argues that the operations of the unaware in the imperial context are different from 'the other'. It does not allow the identities of the coloniser and the colonised to remain fixed and unitary. Colonial power always degrading its own authority and can paradoxically provide the means for native resistance. It not only displaces the history that creates it but establishes new method of authority and generates new kind of political initiatives. It undermines authority because it imitates outwardly only. On account of the difficulty of dividing different cultures into Universalist frameworks, Bhabha evokes an idea of the 'nation' is a little problematic. He thinks that the idea emerges from the imposition of a rather arbitrary 'national' character upon a necessarily very heterogeneous collection of peoples.

Works Cited

Boehmer, Elleke. *Colonial and Postcolonial Literature.* London: OUP, 1995. Print.

Bhabha, Homi. *Location of Culture.* London: Routledge, 1994. Print.

Childs, Peter and Williams, Patric. *An Introduction to Post-colonial Theory.* New York: Harvester Whaetsheaf, 1997. Print.

Chew, Shirley. "Commonwealth Literature." *New Stateman and Society*, 21 July 1995. Print.

Foucault, Michael. *Archeology of Knowledge and Discipline and Punish.* New York: Pantheon Books, 1971. Print.

Hulme, P. "Hurricanes in the Caribbees: The Constitution of the Discourse of English" in F. Barker, P. Hulme, M. Iversen and D. Loxley (eds) *Literature and Power in the Seventeenth Century*. Colchester: University of Essex Press, 1642: 55-83. Print.

Judd, Denis. *Empire: The British Imperial Experience from 1765 to the Present.* England: Harper Collins, 1996. Print.

Jeffares, Norman. *Commonwealth Literature: Unity and Diversity in a Common Culture.* Heinemann: John Press, 1965. Print.

...*Commonwealth Literature:Unity and Diversity in a Common Culture.* Heinemann: John Press, 1965. Print.

Jameson, Frederic. *Postmodernism or, the Cultural Logic of Late Capitalism.* Durham: Duke University Press, 1991. Print.

Loomba, Ania. *Colonialism and Post-Colonialism*. New York: Routledge, 2005. Print.

—.*Colonialism and Post-colonialism*: *The New Critical Idiom*. New York: Routledge, 2005. Print.

Lyotard, D. "Arnold Ferguson, Schiller: Aesthetic culture and the Politics of Aesthetics." *Cultural Critique*, Vol. 2, 1985: 134-69.

—. "Arnold Ferguson, Schiller: Aesthetic culture and the Politics of Aesthetics.' *Cultural Critique*, Vol. 2, 1985: 134-69.

—. "Arnold Ferguson, Schiller: Aesthetic culture and the Politics of Aesthetics'. *Cultural Critique*, Vol. 2, 1985: 134-69.

Memmi, Albert. *Dominated Man: Notes Toward a Portrait.* Orient Press: London, 1968. Print.

—. *Dominated Man: Notes Toward a Portrait.* Orient Press: London, 1968. Print.

—. *Dominated Man: Notes Toward a Portrait.* Orient Press: London, 1968. Print.

—. *Dominated Man: Notes Toward a Portrait.* Orient Press: London, 1968. Print.

Narsimahiah, C. D. *The Swan and the Eagle.* Shimla: IIAS, 1969. Print.

Parry, Benita. *Post-colonial Studies: A Materialistic Critique.* New York: Routledge, 2004.Print.

Mcleod, A. *The Commonwealth Pen: An Introduction to the Literature of the British Commonwealth.* New York: Cornell, 1961. Print.

Rushdie, Salman. *The Midnight's Children.* New York: Avon Books, 1982. Print.

—. *The Midnight's Children.* New York: Avon Books, 1982. Print.

—. *The Midnight's Children.* New York: Avon Books, 1982. Print.

—. *The Midnight's Children.* New York: Avon Books, 1982. Print.

—. and West, Elizabeth. (eds) *The Vintage Book of Indian Writing 1947- 1997.* London: Vintage, 1997. Print.

Spivak, Gayatri. "Can the Subaltern Speak?" *The Postcolonial Studies Reader.* Bill Ashcroft, Gareth, Griffiths and Helen, Tiffin. London: Routledge, 1997: 24-28. Print.

Said, Edward. "Representing the Colonised: Anthropology's Interlocutors." *Critical Inquiry,* Vol. 15, No. 2. 1989. Print.

—. "Orientalism Reconsidered." *Europe and its Others*, Vol.1 July (1984): 234. Print.

—. *Orientalism.* London: Routledge, 1978. Print.

—. *Orientalism.* London: Routledge, 1978. Print.

—. *Orientalism.* London: Routledge, 1978. Print.

—. *Orientalism.* London: Routledge, 1978. Print.

—. *Orientalism.* London: Routledge, 1978. Print.

—. *Orientalism.* London: Routledge, 1978. Print.

—. *Orientalism.* London: Routledge, 1978. Print.

—. *Orientalism.* London: Routledge, 1978. Print.

—. *Orientalism.* London: Routledge, 1978. Print.

—. *Orientalism.* London: Routledge, 1978. Print.

—. *Orientalism.* London: Routledge, 1978. Print.

—. *Orientalism.* London: Routledge, 1978. Print.

—. *Orientalism.* London: Routledge, 1978. Print

White, Patric. *Voss.* New York: Avon, 1957. Print.

Walsh,William. *Commonwealth Literature.* London: OUP, 1973. Print.

Chapter - 2

Indian Literature: An Introduction

The first section of this chapter examines the aspect of evolution of the theme of representation of India in the Indian English novel. Divided into three sections, the first section deals with the origin of the Indian literature and the pre-Independence Indian English novel. The focus is on the prominent novelists and their works. The second section examines the concerns of the Indian English novelists in the post-Independence period and the third section traces the role of the criticism in shaping the thrust of the Indian English fiction.

I

The English education in India introduced by the colonial rulers paved the way for the emergence of Indian English literature. In the beginnings, the novel was imitative of the English novel both in themes and forms. In the subsequent period, nationalism became one of the chief concerns of the Indian English novelists, because of which the genre attracted attention all over the world. R.K. Dhawan writes: it "has attracted widespread interest, both in India and abroad" (Dhawan 5). A good number of Indian writers emerged in the early twentieth century. Ram Mohan Roy who heralded the notion of Indianness was probably aware of what was in store for the Indians in terms of literary awareness. Today "it has won for itself international acclaim and distinction" (Mongia 213).

Ever since the fictional writing has become the most powerful form of literary expression, it occupied a prominent position in Indian English literature. The novel has given a greater literary scope for the exploration of experiences and ideas in the context of our times. Critics and commentators commended greatly the Indian English novels. M. K. Naik writes: "One of the most notable gifts of English education to India is prose fiction for though India was probably a fountain head of story telling, the novel as we know today was an importation form" (Naik 99).

The Indian English literature was initially originated in Bengal state. Later it was found in Madras, Mumbai and the other parts of India. The first Indian novel was Bankim Chandra Chatterjee's *Raj Mohan's Wife* (1864) which paved the way for *Anand Math* (1884), India's first political novel. This novel offered Indians, the National Anthem, "Vande Mataram." Besides, this novel was found to be different when compared to the novels of Durgesh Nandini and Kapal Kandla. Later Manoj Basu's *Jaljangal* has emerged as a prominent translator who has translated *Forest Goddess* by Barindra Nath Bose.

The novels published from the eighteen sixties towards the end of the nineteenth century were written by Bengal and Madras writers. These novels are concerned with the socio-historical and political issues. The first generation of Indian writers started imitating the British writers such as Daniel Defoe, Henry Fielding and Walter Scott to achieve the ease and felicity in English language.

Novels published during 1864 and 1900 include Ram Krishna Punt's *The Bay of Bengal* (1866), Anand Prasad Dutt's *The Indolence* (1878), Shoshee Chunder Dutt's *The Young Zamindar* (1883), Trailokya Das's *Hirimba's Wedding* (1884), Krupabai Satthianandan's *Kamala: A Story of Hindu Child Wife* (1894) and *Saguna: A Story of Native Christian Life* (1895), Michael Madhusudan Dutt's *Bijoy Chand: An Indian Tale* (1888) and Lt. Suresh Biswas: *His Life and Adventures* (1900) and Yogendra Nath Chattopadhyaya's *The Girl and Her Tutor* (1891).

The twentieth century Indian literature became visible with a substantial contribution to the Indian Writing in English. Ramesh Chandra Dutt translated two of his own Bengali novels into English: *The Lake of Palms: A Study of Indian Domestic Life* (1902) and *The Slave Girl of Agra, an Indian Historical Romance* (1909). It is the first realist novel with the objective of exploring social change and its theme was widow remarriages of the Mughal period. Sarath Kumar Ghosh, another Bengali novelist wrote *Verdict of Gods* (1905) and *The Prince of Destiny: The New Krishna* (1909). A. Madhaviah and T. Ramakrishna Pillai, belonging to Madras government, were the two important Bengali novelists. Madhaviah wrote *Satyananda* (1909), *Thrillai Govindan* (1916), *Clarinda* (1915), *Nanda, the Pariah Who Overcame Caste* (1923) and *Lt. Panju-A Modern Indian* (1924). T. Ramakrishna Pillai wrote *Padmini* (1903) and *A Dive for Death* (1911).

Another prominent Indian English Novelist Jogendra Singh hails from Punjab Province. His contribution to the Indian Writing in English is substantial. His fictional work includes: *Nur Jahan,* The Romance of an Indian Queen (1909) and a historical novel*: Nasrin, An Indian Medley* (1911), which presents the realistic aspect of the downfall of the noble life in North India. The first three were published in London and the last one in Lahore. Later novels such as S. T. Ram's *The Cosmopolitan Hindusthani* (1902), L. B. Pal's *A Glimpse of Zanana Life in Bengal* (1904), S. B. Banerjee's *The Adventures of Mrs. Russell* (1909), Balkrishna's *The Love of Kusuma: An Eastern Love Story* (1910), B. K. Sarkar's *Man of Letters* (1911), M. M. Munshi's *Beauty and Joy* (1914) and T. K. Gopal Pannikar's *Storm and Sunshine* (1916) are some other important novels.

The Gandhian movement caught strong support from people across the country during nineteen forties. Consequently, under the influence of Mahatma Gandhi's non-violence movement, the negative political practices disappeared from the scene making new ideas and methods in the political field and every walk of Indian life. The inevitable impact of the Gandhian movement on the Indian English literature was a result of writing realistic novels during the nineteen thirties.

The novelists turned their attention from the past to concentrate on the contemporary issues. Their novels focussed critically on the contemporary social and political problems. The nation-wide movement of Gandhi impelled Indian English novelists providing them with some of the interesting themes such as the struggle for freedom, the East-West encounter, the communal problem, the miserable condition of the untouchables, the landless poor, the downtrodden, the economically exploited and the oppressed.

However, the Gandhian movement with its intense effect on the contemporary events brought a significant difference on the social and political scene of India that can be noticed in K. S. Venkatramani's *Murugan, The Tiller* (1927) and *Kandan, The Patriot: A Novel of New India in the Making* (1932). The former reflects Gandhian economics while the latter reflects his politics. Then came A. S. P. Ayyer, whose novels like *Baladitya* (1930) and *Three Men of Destiny* (1939) are replete with the Gandhian spirit.

II

This section examines the emergence of the literary troika of the Indian English novel and their outstanding contribution to the novel. The arrival of Mulk Raj Anand, R.K. Narayan and Raja Rao on the scene of Indian Writing in English is considered to be the most significant. These novelists embarked upon their writing around the mid 1930s.

The writings of these novelists drifted into the Indian English novel in the right direction. Their writings created an entirely new world, and the Indian novel owes much to their efforts for gaining solid ground and achieving an identity of its own. They were instrumental in making the Indian novel popular. They shaped the concept of character and the nature of the themes which were to give the Indian novel its particular distinctiveness. They "laid the foundation for the genuine Indian English novel, each imparting to the Indian experience a dimension of individuality based on their particular approach to the content and form" (Rao 144).

Mulk Raj Anand (1905-2004) has been the most prolific writer. His contribution to Indian English fiction of social realism is undoubtedly great. His *Untouchable* (1935) presents the story of the low caste boy, Bakha. It is basically a tragic drama of the individual caught in the midst of the age-old caste system. In *Coolie* (1936) he portrays a poverty-stricken protagonist, Munoo. Both the novels are about the downtrodden, the poor and the outcaste, who face economic hardship and humiliation in a rigid social structure (Sing 127). His *Two Leaves and a Bud* (1937) depicts the story of a middle-aged peasant, Ganger, from a village in Punjab.

The other novels of Anand include *The Village* (1939), *Across the Black Waters* (1941), *The Sword and the Sickle* (1942), *The Big Heart* (1945), *Seven Summers* (1951), *The Private Life of Indian Prince* (1953), *The Old Woman and the Cow* (1960), *The Road* (1963), *The Death of the Herd* (1964), *Mourning Face* (1970), *Confession of a Lover* (1976), *The Bubble* (1984), *Little Plays of Mahatma Gandhi* (1998) and *Nine Moods of Bharata, Novel of a Pilgrimage* (1998).

Anand's novels deal with the pitiable condition of the Indian rural society in general and poverty, class, caste system and popular evils of the society in particular. He is one who "believes that literature must serve society, solve their problems and guide them" (Behera 11). He is compared to Charles Dickens regarding the treatment of social themes.

R.K. Narayan (1906-2001) is another greatest Indian novelists in English representing the South Indian Hindu middle class family. He is the lone writer to project the contemporary socio-political issues and reflect the South Indian middle class life in his fiction. He was responsible in creating the fictional imaginary world, 'Malgudi'. The novels published by Narayan during the pre-Independence period include *Swami and Friends* (1935), *The Bachelor of Arts* (1937), *The Dark Room* (1938) and *The English Teacher* (1946).

The art of fictional writing became mature in his novels that appeared after the Independence: *The Financial Expert* (1952), *The Guide* (1958) and *Man Eater of Malgudi* (1962). His other novels include *Waiting for Mahatma* (1955), *The Vendor of Sweets* (1967) and *The Painter of Signs* (1976).

Narayan has four novels to his credit both in the eighties and nineties: *A Tiger for Malgudi* (1983), *Talkative Man* (1983), *The World of Nagaraj* (1990) and *Grandmother's Tale* (1992). Narayan's imaginary fictional world is comparable to Thomas Hardy's 'Wessex.' The people of Malgudi have their local identity by establishing a kinship with all humanity. In his novels, one finds college boys, teachers and taxi drivers of Malgudi. Narayan succeeds in forging a universal vision through his provincial themes. He "peoples in his novels with caricatures rather than characters" (Melwani 31).

Raja Rao (1908-2006), the last of the troika, occupies a pivotal role in Indian writing in English. In this context Azam opines: "Advent on the literary scene has been described as the appearance of a new shinning bright" (Azam 34). His works include *Kanthapura* (1938), *The Serpent and the Rope* (1960), *The Cat and Shakespeare* (1965), *Comrade Kirillov* (1976) and *The Chessmaster and His Moves* (1988). *Kanthapura* is probably the first finest representation of the Gandhian movement in Indian English fiction. It is about the story of a village examining the Gandhian ideology of non-violence and abolition of untouchability.

The Serpent and the Rope, which won the Sahitya Academy Award in 1963, is considered a landmark in Indian English fiction. Its technique presents a successful orchestration of the Indian and Western methods. *The Cat and the Shakespeare*, a metaphysical comedy, is an example of philosophical fiction. *The Chessmaster and His Moves* is characterised by an array of meaningful symbols. Raja Rao's place in the realm of Indian English fiction is safe as a stylist, symbolist, myth-maker, the finest painter of the East-West encounter and a philosophical novelist.

The literary troika contributed to the Indian writing in English substantially. Their fictional writings have dealt with the socio-economic and political conditions of India. In addition to these writers, the Muslim novelists depicted in their works the life in Muslim households. They include: Ahmed Ali's *Twilight in Delhi* (1940) and *Ocean of Night* (1964), Iqbalunnisa Hussain's *Purdah and Polygamy*: Life in an Indian Muslim Household (1944), Humayun Kabir's *Men and River* (1945), a novel based on a folk tale, Amir Ali's *Conflict* (1947), *Via Geneva* (1967) and *Assignment in Kashmir* (1973), K. A. Abbas's *Tomorrow is Ours:* A Novel of the India of Today (1943) and *Inquilab*: A Novel of the Indian Revolution (1955).

Among others who deserve mention are: Dhan Gopal Mukherji's four novels: *Kari, The Elephant (1922), Hari, the Jungle Lad (1924),*

The Chief of the Herd (1929), and Ghond, the Hunter (1929). C. S. Rau's *The Confessions of a Bogus Patriot* (1923), Ram Narain's *Tigress of the Herem* (1930), Chintamani's *Vedantam or the Clash of Traditions* (1938), Shankar Ram's *Love of Dust* (1938), D. F. Karaka's *Just Flesh* (1941), *There Lay the City* (1942) and *We Never Die* (1944), C. N. Zutshi's *Motherland* (1944), Purushottamdas Tricumdas's *Living Mask* (1947).

In the post-Independence era, India had to overcome many challenges as it faced the problems related to social, political, economic and cultural spheres. In due course of time, India acquired an identity of its own through Indian writing English. It generated in the writer self-confidence, broad thinking and sharpened his self-examining ability. As a result of these developments, the literary avenues were registered, particularly in fiction, poetry and criticism. Fiction is already well established and raised both in variety and stature.

The convention of social realism in Indian English fiction used by Mulk Raj Anand flourished during the nineteen fifties and early sixties through Bhabani Bhattacharya, Manohar Malgonkar and Khushwant Singh. Sudhin Ghosh, G.V. Desani and Anantanarayanan enlivened the trend of the experimental novel, oriented by Raja Rao in his *Kanthapura*. In addition, the fictional works of B. Rajan present the combined effect of realism and fantasy.

Bhabani Bhattacharya's fiction explores social purpose, as he believes that the "novel must have a social purpose" (Khatri 60). He sporadically succeeded in achieving the succinct interpretation of life. In his first novel *So Many Hungers* (1947), Bhattacharya explores the theme of exploitation on the political, economic and social front during the Quit India movement and the Bengal Famine of the early 1940s. He continued the tradition of social realism stressing, like Anand, the necessity of social purpose in fiction. In *Music for Mohini* (1952) Bhattacharya shows the age-old vision of life with the new semi-western attitude.

In *He Who Rides the Tiger* (1952), Bhattacharya forms an idea of complicated criss-cross of themes such as appearance and reality, the rich and the poor and religious hypocrisy. His *Goddess Named*

Gold (1960) is the finest example of allegorical writing. In *Shadow from Ladakh* (1966), he applied symbolism against the background of the Chinese invasion of 1962. In *A Dream in Hawaii* (1978), he presents the theme of the East-West encounter. Bhattacharya's significant contribution to Indian English fiction is substantial. He is "the only Indian English writer whose work has been translated into over two dozen foreign languages" (Melwani 31).

Manohar Malgonkar, one of the famous Indian English novelists of the modern era, started his writing career after the Independence with the publication of *Distant Drum* (1960). He is an artist of the first order. He achieves feasibility in literary sensibility and critical maturity. He "subtly makes a landmark as a historical novelist" (Kumar 105). Although is a realist, Malgonkar believes that art has no other purpose to serve than pure entertainment. But his major work is obsessed with the role of history in the individual and social life.

Distant Drum is a documentary of army life in its different aspects and a celebration of army code as developed by the Britishers. *Combat of Shadows* (1962) extracts its title and epigraph from the *Bhagvad Gita*. *The Princess* (1963) is considered the best political novel by Malgonkar. It reveals the greatness of the princely world. The setting of *A Bend in the Ganges* (1964) is about the Partition and the *Ramayana* is the source of its title and epigraph. *The Devil's Wind* (1972) examines the great Revolt of 1857.

His novels after 1980 include *Bandicoot Run* (1982), *The Garland Keepers* (1987) and *Cactus Country* (1992) with spy tales as central to the novel. Khushwant Singh appears on the scene as a realist with the publication of *Train to Pakistan* (1956). Singh depicts the impact of partition on a small village on the India-Pakistan border. His second novel *I Shall Not Hear the Nightingale* (1959) gives an ironic picture of a Sikh joint family symbolising different Indian reactions to the freedom movement of the 1940s. His later novels include *Delhi* (1990) and *The Company of Women* (1999).

Another novelist of the period is J. Menon Marath, whose realism is deeply rooted in his native land, Kerala. He wrote *Wound of Spring* (1960), *The Sale of an Island* (1968) and *Janu* (1988). Bhalachandra Rajan presents a blend of realism and fantasy, the two conspicuous strains in the Indian English fiction of the nineteen fifties and sixties. Unlike his contemporaries, Rajan's realism is less social than psychological which is clear from his first novel, *The Dark Dancer* (1959).

His second novel *Too Long in the West* (1961) is a comic extravaganza. Another novelist, Sudhindra Nath Ghosh adopts the ancient native tradition of story-telling to express the Indian ethos in all of his four novels: *And Gazelles Leaping* (1949), *Cradle of the Clouds* (1951), *The Vermilion Boat* (1953) and *The Fame of the Forest* (1955). G.V. Desani's *All About H. Hatter* (1948) is an experimental novel. In presenting the story of the hero's search for a viable philosophy of living and his quest for understanding the meaning of life, Desani blends Indian and Western narrative forms.

An important feature of this period was the emergence of Indian women novelists writing in English adding a new dimension to Indian English novel especially after the Independence. Important of them include Ruth Prawer Jhabvala, Kamala Markandaya, Nayantara Sahgal and Anita Desai. Kamala Markandaya is one of the most outstanding and significant Indian English novelists. Her novels are suffused with a rich variety of settings, characters and themes. Her first novel *Nectar in a Sieve* (1954) is about the troubles and tribulations of a peasant couple, Nathan and Rukmani of a South Indian Village. Her second novel, *Some Inner Fury* (1957) is a political novel exploring the burden of human relationships in the wake of Quit India Movement. *A Silence of Desire* (1961) depicts the conflict between the Indian spiritual faith and modernism born of India's association with the West. *Possession* (1963) appears to be a continuation of *A Silence of Desire* which is based on the conflict between Indian spiritualism and Western materialism.

Two of her later novels, *A Handful of Rice* (1966) and *Two Virgins* (1973) depict the modernism brought in by the Western influences, which inspire the protagonists to revolt against their traditional environment, and seek their fulfillment by shaping their careers independently.

In *The Coffer Dams* (1969) Markandeya juxtaposes the theme of the East-West encounter from a different angle by presenting the conflict between technological powers. She exposes a new dimension of the theme of East-West confrontation in *The Nowhere Man* (1972) revealing the predicament of Indian immigrants in England. For the first time, she tries her pen at historical fiction with the publication of *The Golden Honeycomb* (1977), a chronicle of three generations of the princely family of Devpur. Her next novel was *Pleasure City* (1982). Markandeya treats the theme of East-West confrontation more comprehensively than any other Indian English novelists.

Another woman novelist, Ruth Prawer Jhabvala takes up the concept of arranged marriages in India and presents an ironic survey of the East-West confrontation. Her early novels *To Whom She Will* (1955) and *The Nature of Passion* (1956) are exquisite comedies of urban middle-class life in nineteen fifties and sixties. Her other novels *The Householder* (1960), *Get Ready for Battle* (1962), *A New Dominion* (1973), *Heat and Dust* (1975), *In Search of Love and Beauty* (1983), *The Continents* (1987), *Poet and Dancer* (1993) and *Shards of Memory* (1995) examine keenly the strangeness of human behaviour presenting gentle irony and good humoured satire.

Nayantara Sahgal, who excels in portraying the theme of political novel in India, writes simple prosaic tales about politicians and bureaucrats. In addition to the explicit political theme, Sahgal shows her preoccupation with the modern Indian woman's search for sexual freedom and self-realisation, and her novels include *A Time to be Happy* (1958), *This Time of Morning* (1968), *Storm in Chandigarh* (1969), *The Day in Shadow* (1971), *A Situation in New Delhi* (1977), *Rich Like Us* (1985), *Plans for Departure* (1985) and *Mistaken Identity* (1988).

After the 1960s, the Indian English fiction shifted its attention from the public life to the private life. The sophisticated war-weaponry used in Second World War has caused human destruction across the world. It has led to mental retardation, psychological disorders and loss of moral values.

The Indian novelists did not remain aloof from the contemporary situations. Instead of dealing with the exploration and the interpretation of social problems, they deal with the subjects of human existence and quest for identity in all its manifestations. The novelists like Anita Desai and Arun Joshi who explored the predicament of modern man's life "changed the face of Indian English novel" (Verma 1).

Anita Desai is one of the contemporary Indian women novelists portraying the tragedy of human life "interested in the interior landscape of the mind than in political and social realities" (Iyer 176). Having a flair for writing, she projects the predicament of the modern man. Her themes are particularly concerned with the depiction of practical and social realities of life. Desai is very much influenced by the great philosophers of the west and the fast changing elements in the social structure of India. Loneliness being her main theme, *Cry, the Peacock* (1963), *Voices in the City* (1965) and *Bye-Bye Blackbird* (1997) are representative of her concerns.

Her famous novel *Where Shall We Go this Summer* won the Akademi Award in the year 1975. This novel explores Sita's awareness of a basic confusion in the urban life, between compassion and the odour of death and destruction. "It depicts the inner outer world of its protagonist Sita and her fatigue for life" (Prasad 112). In *Clear Light of Day* (1980), she presents an ironic parallel between the freedom of the country and Raja's and Bhima's own personal freedom. Her *Fire on the Mountain* (1999) delineates the similar existential predicament of the individuals.

Towards the end of the sixties and early seventies, Chaman Nahal and Arun Joshi occupy an important place. Arun Joshi discusses modern man's psychological trauma, as noted by a critic: "it is with the novels of Arun Joshi and Anita Desai that a new era in the Indian English fiction began and also witnessed a change in the treatment of themes" (Bhatt and Alexandra 11).

Joshi occupies a premier position among the major Indian English novelists of the twentieth century. He was exceptionally perceptive as a creative artist. His premature death in 1993 abruptly ended his promising literary career. His novels include *The Foreigner* (1968), *The Strange Case of Billy Biswas* (1971), *The Apprentice* (1974), *The Last Labyrinth* (1981), *The City and the River* (1990) and a collection of short stories, *The Survivor* (1975). There is also a work of biography entitled *Lala Shri Ram: A Study in Entrepreneurship in Industrial Management* (1975), which is more in the nature of domestic eulogy. He won the prestigious Sahitya Akademi Award for his fourth novel *The Last Labyrinth* in 1982.

Chaman Nahal is a famous Indian novelist among the contemporary writers of Joshi. His most outstanding works before the eighties was *Azadi* (1975), one of the most prominent novels on the theme of Partition. His other novels include *My True Faces* (1973), *Into another Dawn* (1977) and *The English Queens* (1979), *The Crown and The Lioncloth* (1981), *The Salt of Life* (1990) and *The Triumph of the Tricolour* (1993).

After 1980s, new writing emerged to sustain the Indian writing in English. The novelists such as Salman Rushdie, Vikram Seth, Upmanyu Chatterjee, Shashi Deshpande, Shashi Tharoor, Shobha De, Amitav Ghose, Amit Choudhary, Arundhati Roy, Kiran Desai and Aravind Adiga are the most prominent novelists. Shashi Deshpande is a distinguished novelist with sustained achievement. She has eight novels to her credit. Her themes include exploring a solution for the identity crisis of the modern women in her works *The Dark Holds No Terrors* (1980), *If I Die Today* (1982), *A Matter of Times* (1996) and *Small Remedies* (2000).

Amitav Ghosh, one of the most popular names in recent Indian English fiction, started with *The Circle of Reason* (1986) followed by *In An Antique Land* (1992), *The Calcutta Chromosome* (1996) and *The Glass Palace* (2000). Shashi Tharoor's first novel *The Great Indian Novel* (1989) is one of the finest examples of post-modern fiction.

Vikram Seth published a novel in verse, *The Golden Gate*, in 1986. In 1993 his much acclaimed novel *A Suitable Boy*, won him great fame. It was followed by *An Equal Music* (1999). Amit Choudhary published four novels, namely A *Strange and Sublime Address* (1991), *Afternoon Raag* (1993), *Freedom Song* (1998) and *A New World* (2000).

Another writer of immense significance is Arundhati Roy, who won the Booker Prize for her maiden novel, *The God of Small Things*

(1997). It is a tale of shock and horror with the theme of death and decay. Roy confides immorality in public life, which is rocked by party politics and selfish motives.

Salman Rushdie's *Midnight's Children* (1981) signifies a new era in the history of Indian English Fiction. His other important novels include *Shame* (1983) and *Satanic Verses* (1988). Arundhati Roy's *The God of Small Things* occupies a special significance in the lineage of the recent Indian English fiction. Kiran Desai emerged as a famous literary figure in Indian writing in English with her two novels: *Hullabaloo in the Guava Orchard* (1998) and *The Inheritance of Loss* (2006), which won the Booker Prize. She explores in the novel the Indian history in a significant way. Aravind Adiga's *The White Tiger* (2007) is another novel that won the Man Booker prize for 2007. He projects the modern Indian socio-economic situation in the globalised world.

The Indian English novel has undergone tough times in terms of publication in the beginning. There was a time when Mulk Raj Anand's *Untouchable* was left untouched by British publishers before being recommended by E. M. Foster to Lawrence and Wishart to accept it. Same thing happened to R.K. Narayan's *Swami and Friends*, which had to wait for Graham Greene's recommendation. But presently, the Indian English novel is now readily accepted abroad. The Indian English novel has gained a unique recognition, vibrancy and vitality attracting a remarkable acclaim.

An attempt to understand the historical fiction, which is the main thrust of the research, would help to understand the novels selected for the study. History in general is understood in terms of the political history, which is based on the names of kings and monarchs and the details pertaining to who succeeded whom and how at a particular point of time.

In more recent times, it is understood to engage with constitutional changes and the power politics behind them. However, it is not easy to define and describe the nature and subject of history in order to get a comprehensive idea of any particular period of time. It is necessary to take into account religions, inventions, warfare, expansion of trade and cultural and economical activities. Juliet Gardiner describes history as "an unending dialogue between the present and the past" (Gardner 1).

Arthur Marwick shows three levels of history in his work: first, it can indicate the whole human past as it actually happened. Second, history suggests man's attempt to describe and interpret the past. The latter comes nearer to the original Greek meaning "inquiry." The third meaning indicates the systematic study of history as a scientific discipline (Marwick 15). Macaulay however treats history differently. He holds that history "falls alternately under the sole of an absolute dominion of both reason and imagination. It is sometimes fiction and sometimes theory" (Macaulay 72).

III

Literary criticism can be both critical and supportive of a genre. The Indian English literary criticism played a significant role not only in shaping the genre, but also in giving a thrust and direction to the representation of India in the genre. Most noteworthy of them are Srinivasa Iyengar, C.D. Narsimahiah, Meenakshi Mukherjee, M.K. Naik, among others. Mukherjee, who played an instrumental role in the appreciation of the genre, concludes her *Twice Born Fiction*: "Indian English fiction, which has served for so long as a file or document of sociology of anthropology or educational theory must now be regarded as literature and evaluated as such. That is the service it requires from critics, and this study is a modest essay in this direction" (Mukherjee 210).

K.R. Srinivasa Iyengar contributed immensely to the criticism of the Indian English writing in contrast to other critics such as David Mc Cutchion, who were critical of the genre. Mc Cutchion for example is very harsh towards the Indian English novelists. His analysis of the Indian English fiction is that in the novels moods are invoked of sadness and fantasy. Murli Das Melwani is yet another critic who attacked the genre. He writes that an Indian English novelist is always in search of subjects and critics.

According to him, none seems to have grappled yet with the new and exciting India of the fifties, sixties and seventies. M.K. Naik is a midway between the sympathisers and the bitter critics of the Indian English fiction. He says that the trends in recent fiction unmistakably indicate how the new novelists are trying to tread fresh paths and this is the surest sign of the continued vitality of an art though actual achievement is naturally determined by many factors including genius.

Paul Verghese, a Marxist critic, praises the Indian English novels for opting 'Humanism' and 'hunger' as their themes. Chalapati Rai is very caustic when he remarks that writing is close to life, but the Indian English novels have little to do with life. Uma Parameswaran, who criticised Indian English fiction earlier in pessimistic tone in the seventies, now, appreciates Salman Rushdie for his novel *Midnight's Children*. Saros Cowasjee, Kirpal, R.K. Dhawan, William Walsh, P.S. Sundaram, R.S. Singh, Balram Das Gupta, Harish Razda, E.J. Kalinnikova, R.S. Pathak, R.K. Singh, K.K. Sharma and others are supportive of the Indian English novels.

The next chapter attempts to examine the history and politics of the Man Booker Prize for a better understanding of the novels selected for the study.

Works Cited

Azam, S. M. R. "Ambiguity in Raja Rao's Second Novel: *The Serpent and The Rope*." *Indian Novel in English: Critical Perspective*. Ed. Prasad Amar Nath New Delhi: Sarup and Sons, 2000. Print.

Arthur, Marwick. *The Nature of History*. London: OUP, 1967. Print.

Behera, Smruti Ranjan. "The Literary Style of Mulk Raj Anand." *Indian Writing in English*. Vol. III. New Delhi: Atlantic Publishers and Distributors, 1999. Print.

Bhatt, Indira and Alexander, Suja. *Arun Joshi's Fiction: A Critique*. New Delhi: Creative Books, 2001. Print.

Dhawan, R.K, ed. *The Fictional World of Arun Joshi*. New Delhi: Classical Publishing Company, 1986. Print.

—. *The Fictional World of Arun Joshi*. New Delhi: Classical Publishing Company, 1986.Print.

Macaulay, D.B. "History and Literature." *The Varieties of History*. Ed. Fritz Stern. New York: The Word Publishing Company, 1970. Print.

Iyer, N. Sharada. "The Blackbird's Rough Passage." *Indian English Literature*. Vol. II. Ed. Naikar. New Delhi: Atlantic Publishers and Distributors, 2002. Print.

Juliet, Gardiner. "Introduction. *What is History Today?*" Ed. Juliet Gardiner. London: Macmillan Education, 1986. Print.

Khatri, Chhote Lal. "Bhabani Bhattacharya's *He Who Rides a Tiger: A Socio-Economic Perspective.*" *Studies in Indian Writing in English.* Vol. I. Ed. Rajeshwar and Piciucco. New Delhi: Atlantic Publishers and Distributors, 2000. Print.

Kumar, Arjun. "Manohar Malgonkar's Novels: A True Dynamo of Historical Sense and Sensibility." *Indian English Literature.* Vol. II. Ed. Naikar. New Delhi: Atlantic Publishers and Distributors, 2002. Print.

Mongia, Sunanda. "Recent Indian Fiction in English: An Overview." *Spectrum History of Indian Literature in English.* Ed. Singh Ram Sewak and Singh Charu Sheel. New Delhi: Atlantic Publishers and Distributors, 1997. Print.

Melwani, Murli Das. *Themes in Indian English Literature.* Bareilly: Prakash Book Depot, 1977. Print.

Mukherji, Meenakshi. *Twice Born Fiction.* Atlantic Publishers and Distributors, 2002. Print.

Naik, M. K. *Dimensions of Indian English Literature.* New Delhi: Sterling Publishers, 1985. Print.

Prasad, Amar Nath. *Indian Novel in English: Critical Perspective.* New Delhi: Sarup and Sons, 2000. Print.

Rao, K. R. *The Fiction of Raja Rao.* Aurangabad: Parimal Prakashan, 1980. Print.

Singh, Ram Sewak and Singh, Charu, Sheel, Eds. *Spectrum History of Indian Literature in English.* New Delhi: Atlantic Publishers and Distributors, 1997. Print.

Verma, Mukesh Rajan. "Indian English Novel since 1985." *Reflections on Indian English Literature.* Ed. M.R. and K.A. Agarwal. New Delhi: Atlantic Publishers and Distributors, 2002. Print.

Chapter - 3

Canon: The Role of the Booker

Ever since the beginning of written literature, the privileging of some writers over the other writers has been in place in subtle forms. During the feudal period, writers used to be handpicked by the ruling classes for patronisation. In turn, the writers used their skill and writing for eulogising the rulers. Literary prizes or titles used to be offered by rulers, monarchs and other patrons who "cannily deployed them for the double purpose of proving their munificence while reconfirming the loyalty of their subjects" (Winegarten 65). The ruler-writer nexus had thus been reciprocal. With the emergence of the capital playing an important role in the promotion of arts and literature, literary awards and prizes took the role of the patronisation of the writers. The patronisation, awards, prizes and other forms of promotion of the authors have been different forms of privileging select writers, which in the present context could be termed the canonisation. This chapter seeks to explore the aspect of the Booker Prize as an important form of canonisation of the novelists both from the former coloniser—England—and the former colonies, against the backdrop of post-colonial literary writing.

The literary prizes have been instituted in order to promote the literary works and authors. Especially the British private companies have come forward to institute several cash prizes to honour the writers. Among the prizes and awards, the Man Booker Prize has been next to the Nobel Prize for literature. Started in 1969, it was first sponsored by the Booker McConnell Company. The award subsequently became known as the Man Booker prize in 2002 when the investment company Man Group began to sponsor the award. The prize is awarded annually to a writer from the British Commonwealth or the Republic of Ireland writing in the English language. The winner is chosen by a panel of judges, largely constituting prominent writers, critics and members of the publishers.

The literary prizes are greatly seen as a fact of the late nineteenth and twentieth centuries since the patrons have supported with a credible emphasis on public sponsorship. The global cultural economy is controlled by the big multinational companies. As a result, the corporate sponsorship of the arts has become an undeniable fact. The corporate prize, like the endowed Chair, is a 'gift' that makes publicity to the company while working as a figurative indicator of its authorising power. Since the state subsidies of the arts have lessened in many countries, the corporate sponsors have emerged to govern the literary/artistic scene.

However, corporate sponsorship has largely overtaken the earlier, predominantly hierarchical systems of private and public patronage. The ideas of literature and literary value were upheld (Bourdieu 4). The evaluative process for corporate sponsorship differs a lot and it would clearly be misguided to see it as a uniform regime (Appadurai 4). It is a painful thing to underestimate historical trajectory that each sponsoring agency follows.

Literary prizes and awards are not free from controversies. Huggan writes: "Such awards have come out with controversies, many of them in the later twentieth century, as a response to the globalisation of, especially English language-literature" (Huggan 106). This aspect influences the production and consumption of world literature in English. Berth Lindfors opines: "The most famous of all international literary awards, the Nobel, established in 1901, has had a distinctly Eurocentric bias since its inception" (Lindfors 222). This is true of the corporate awards like the Booker. Hig Eakin suggests: "The booker, despite its multicultural consciousness has arguably done less to further the development of non-western and post-colonial literatures than it has to encourage the commerce of an "exotic" commodity catered to the western literary market" (Eakin 1).

The history of the prize involved conflicts ever since the Prize had been instituted. Tom Maschler, for instance, writes: "The prize took its inspiration from the then better known French pix Goncourt, a hierarchy since arguably reversed, with *Le Figaro* describing the Goncourt as the French Booker" (Maschler 15-16). It is originally established as a $5,000 award to the best full length English language novel of the year. The prize has got enthusiastic response. It is in fact considered one of the world famous literary prizes.

Meticulous care is being taken in terms of media management to protect its prestige. Hermione Lee suggests in this regard: "Ensured that Booker (will) forever be identified by the word "razzmattaz," playing up to its vulgar Miss World aspect and mixing in the British eye a peculiar view of writers as dinner-jacketed gormandizers" (Lee VII). Sir Michael Caine, former Chairman of Booker private limited company and the Prize Management committee is equally cynical in noting the costs involved in attracting such high level publicity: "At first, the Management Committee organised both the award procedures and the ceremony. Gradually, the economy and its form become a wholly Booker matter. The costs bear this out" (Caine 9).

The Booker is a meticulously organised media event. It succeeded in drawing required attention and hype in the media. Further, it generates debates and arguments about the literary controversies. Todd sums up the controversies: "The time lag between the announcement of the shortlist and the declaration of the winner successfully generates suspense while maximising missing commercial appear" (Todd 63).

The important stakeholders of the awards that include the publishers vie with each other to re-print the award winning novels. The Prize winners are often assured of huge advances and commercial success. Consequently, the advances paid to the Booker Prize winning novels increased multifold, which continues to be paid for the subsequent books.

TV and Film rights have emerged in order to get the writers' consent for producing serials and films on the award winning works. For example, Michael Ondaatje, whose novel *The English Patient*

(1996), has been made into the film. This kind of media hype made the Booker much more popular than its counterparts: "All in all, there can be no doubt that, the booker more than any other prize in recent history, has got enthusiastic response in the commercialisation of English Language literature" (Huggan 108). As the monetary reward increases, the prize exerts a major influence over the cultural perceptions as well as the reading habits of its consumer public.

Merritt Moseley writes: "The Booker prize exercises an immense influence on the publishing world; and more surprisingly, on the minds and enthusiasms of people well outside that world, which by the American standards is impossible" (Mosley 613). The economic aspect and the media publicity reached the unacceptable levels and the prize has been recognised as a "wonderful marketing idea" (Moseley 613).

Another aspect of the controversy about the Booker has been the prejudice and preference of the jury of the award. The judges are variedly accused of nepotism, chauvinism and pretty squabbling. There is a criticism that the judges have crucially taken the seat of judgement in favour of the British. Consequently, it results in a strong belief among the readers that the discredited view is widely spread over in commonwealth fictions.

Critics accused the authors as angling for a prize or looking for the commercial aspect. Individual selections have been singled out by the media as a catastrophe. For example, Keri Hume's Moari Novel *The Borne People*, a controversial winner of Booker prize in 1985 is considered favourite in spite of its critical acclaim and its relative commercial success.

The individual authors have been criticised for obscurity or obscenity as in the case of James Kelman, who won the Booker prize for *How Late it was, How Late* in 1994. It attracted reviews that spluttered with wrath. John Berger was awarded the Booker in 1972 for his scandalous experimental novel, and he continued to cause further: "scandal by donating half his prize-money to the militant Black Panther movement on the humanitarian grounds as he said in his acceptance speech is covered up as an 'embarrassment" (Goff 11-23).

A source of controversy surrounding the Booker has been the authors themselves. Salman Rushdie, the Booker Prize winner in 1981 for *Midnight's Children* lined up for yet another Booker for his *Shame*. When he failed to get it, Rushdie expressed his anger and dissent. He described Coetzee's *Life and Times of Michael* "shitty winner" (Huggan 109). Such criticism is subjective and is indicative of the negative impact that the media hype created. This kind of criticism is highly biased. Todd views: "A word is required for getting the eligibility criteria on the involvement of a noticeable shift from English literature to English language literature published in Britain" (Todd 96).

In his book *Consuming Fictions* (1996), Richard Todd writes that the Booker Prize played an important role in creating awareness of global aspects of English language fiction: "The Unprecedented exposure of fiction from English speaking countries other than the United Kingdom or the United States led to an increasingly global picture of fiction in Britain during the course of the 1980s or 1990s. Booker short list is not centered on Britain" (Todd 83).

Todd has globally pictured the fictional writing in an advanced level by replacing the conventional view of a commonwealth of literary nations. Pico Iyer explores that the post-colonial awareness is seemingly stated by internationally reputed prizes like the Booker. Iyer considers Salman Rushdie's *Midnight's Children* (1981) as a watershed novel in the emergence of the post-colonial literary era. The Prize, since Rushdie won it, has gone to "two Australians, a part Maori, A South African, a woman of polish descendent and an exile from Japan. Runners up have featured such redoubtably English names as Mo and Mistry and Achebe, when a traditional English name takes the prize.

Iyer perceives that the writers from the commonwealth countries are 'writing back.' A new breed of writing from the erstwhile commonwealth countries has emerged to compete with Britain's canonical writers. The post-colonial for Iyer is the code word for these transnational operations: "It describes both the impetus toward anti-imperial struggle and the deliberation of a cultural pluralism that cannot be contained within national boundaries" (Huggan 24).

The positive role played by Booker Prize has been acquiring legitimacy to the post-colonial writing. The exoticist has provided the constructive in an objectification way. The English language and literature results in a variety of commercially successful writing of the colonial other: "This fetishisation of cultural otherness risks merely reduplicating the authority of the assimilationist paradigms that such multicultural writing apparently seeks to replace" (Huggan 111). The Booker is seemingly seen as a focus on the Anglo-centric discourse of the benevolent paternalism.

The Booker Prize is also seen as endorsing the British cultural pluralism. The Judges endeavour to maintain critical balance: "whether the prize might not be some form or other of affirmative action for marginal literatures" (Eakin 6).

These serious discussions are basically about the themes of the novels: "One such theme, sometimes considered to be a gauge of the Booker's post-colonial leanings, is *revisionist* history. More than half of the prize winning novels to date investigate aspects of primarily colonial, history or present a counter-memory to the official historical record" (Huggan 111).

II

This section is aimed at problematising the four select novels in the context of the Booker Prizes. The literary prizes in general function as legitimising mechanisms that foreground the symbolic as well as the material effects of the process of literary evaluation. The four Indian novels, which have been selected for the study, have undergone a meticulously evaluated process before being awarded the Man Booker Prize.

Salman Rushdie's *Midnight's Children*, Arundhati Roy's *The God of Small Things,* Kiran Desai's *The Inheritance of Loss* and Aravind Adiga's *The White Tiger* represent a particular aspect of India in each of them. The awarding of the Booker Prize to each of the four novels in turn helped acquire legitimacy at international level to what the novels represent as themes.

With Salman Rushdie's *Midnight's Children* being awarded the Booker, the Indian writing in English became more visible in terms of readership, criticism, theory and the media hype. Rushdie became a model for emulation in the subsequent period. With the Booker, Salman Rushdie became an acclaimed literary figure in the post-colonial era. A major post-colonial writer, Rushdie's works are replete with the immigrant outlook.

Being aware of his Indian ancestry, Rushdie takes up historic allusions in his works. Having been conferred around twenty five literary awards, three honorary awards, the Booker Prize for *Midnight's Children* in 1981, Booker of the Bookers in 1993 and also Best of Booker for the same in 2008, the first Booker catapulted Rushdie to the world stage as a novelist of significance. The Booker Prize thus projects a particular author disproportionately. It helps legitimise an author and promote him for a wider readership. Consequently, the subject matter that the Booker Prize novel represents also gets legitimacy.

Arundhati Roy's *The God of Small Things*, second Indian Booker Prize winning novel, similarly took the post-colonial literary world by storm. Set in a small village in Kerala, the novel deals with the story of one particular family. Replete with the social aspects vis-à-vis the Dalit suppression and women suppression, the novel explores the social, economical and political conditions of India.

Though the novel looks simple, a close reading of the novel reveals that it is a well planned work and has a subtle and complex plot. Composed of memories treated artistically, the events are absorbing and interesting. The Booker to *The God of Small Things* helped in acquiring legitimacy to the significance of the local, which Roy makes global in the novel.

Kiran Desai, the third Indian novelist to have received the Booker Prize is yet another writer who has been canonised as a writer. Kiran Desai, as a daughter of famous Indian novelist Anita Desai, found it easy to be known among the readers because of the prize as well as the lineage. *The Inheritance of Loss*, which won the coveted Booker in 2006, the novel is set partly in India and partly in the U.S. Exploring the consequences of the introduction of the Western element into a non-western country, the novel explores the aspect of the nuanced forms of the colonialism in the post-colonial context.

Writing about the immigrant experience in New York, Desai realises that she would have to return to India. Having returned to India, she wrote about Kalimpong. This explains why her description of both Kalimpong and Darjeeling come across as something authentic. The same is true about the political information provided in the novel. In Kiran's India, people are inflicted of the incurable poverty and privation. The minds of the people are filled with anguish and anger because of the non-fulfillment of their basic needs resulting in terrorist violence. On the other hand, there are people who want to leave the country because of poverty, backwardness and lack of opportunities.

The fourth Indian Booker Prize novel, Aravind Adiga's *The White Tiger* has been yet another work that attracted both applause and criticism. Dealing with the life of one Balram Halwai, who immediately catches our imagination, the novel is a kind of a tale of two Indias. Balram's journey from the darkness of village life to the light of entrepreneurial success is utterly amoral, brilliantly irreverent, deeply endearing and altogether unforgettable. This novel juxtaposes globalised India where the developmental activity has come to a standstill due to the corrupt people of India.

The following four chapters, devoted to the examination of Salman Rushdie's *Midnight's Children*, Arundhati Roy's *The God of Small Things,* Kiran Desai's *The Inheritance of Loss* and Aravind Adiga's *The White Tiger* will focus on four different aspects of India.

Works Cited

Bourdieu, P. *The Field of Cultural Production: Essays on Art and Literature.* Ed. R. Johnson. New York: Columbia University Press, 1993. Print.

—. *The Field of Cultural Production: Essays on Art and Literature.* Ed. R. Johnson. New York: Columbia University Press, 1993. Print.

Caine, Sir M.H. "The Booker Story, *Booker 30: A Celebration of 30 Years of the Booker Prize for Fiction* 1969–1998" St. Ives: Booker, 1998. Print.

Eakin, H. 'Literary Prizes in the Age of Multi-culturalism,' unpublished Research Paper, Harvard University Print, 1995. Print.

Goff, M. 'Introduction' M.Goff (ed.). *Prize Writing: An Original Collection of Writings by Past Winners to Celebrate 21 Years of the Booker Prize.* London: Hodder and Stoughton, 1989.Print.

—."How the Booker Prize Works." Online source: http://www.bookerprize.co.uk/site/fact/about/aboutfset_pw.html.2000.Web.15 Nov. 2011.

Huggan, Graham. *The Postcolonial Exotic: Marketing and Margins.* London: Taylor and Francis Group, 2001. Print.

—. *The Postcolonial Exotic*: Marketing and Margins. London: Taylor and Francis Group, 2001. Print.

—. *The Postcolonial Exotic*: Marketing and Margins.London: Taylor and Francis Group, 2001. Print.

—. *The Postcolonial Exotic*: Marketing and Margins. London: Taylor and Francis Group, 2001. Print.

Huggins, J. and Huggins, R. *Auntie Rita.* Canberra: Australian Institute of Aboriginal Studies, 1994. Print.

Iyer, P. "The Empire Writes Back." *Time,* 8 February, 1993. Print.

—. "The Empire Writes Back." *Time,* 8 February, 1993. Print.

Lindfors, B. (ed.) *Dem-Say: Interviews with Eight Nigerian Writers,* Austin. TX: African and Afro-American Studies and Research Center, University of Texas at Austin, 1974. Print.

Maschler, T. "How It All Began in *Booker 30: A Celebration of 30 Years of the Booker Prize for Fiction."* St Ives: Booker, 1969–1998. Print.

Moseley, M. "Britain's Booker Prize." *Sewanee Review.* 4 April, 1993: 613–23. Print.

Todd, R. *Consuming Fictions: The Booker Prize and Fiction in Britain Today.* London: Bloomsbury, 1996. Print.

—. *Consuming Fictions: The Booker Prize and Fiction in Britain Today.* London: Bloomsbury, 1996. Print.

—. *Consuming Fictions: The Booker Prize and Fiction in Britain Today.* London: Bloomsbury, 1996. Print.

—. *Consuming Fictions: The Booker Prize and Fiction in Britain Today.* London: Bloomsbury, 1996. Print.

Walsh, W., ed. *A Manifold Voice: Studies in Commonwealth Literature.* London: Chatto and Windus, 1970. Print.

—. *A Manifold Voice: Studies in Commonwealth Literature.* London: Chatto and Windus, 1970. Print.

Winegarten, R. "The Nobel Prize for Literature." *American Scholar* 63, 1.1994. Print.

Chapter - 4

The Personal and the Public: History in *Midnight's Children*

This chapter examines the representation of history in *Midnight's Children* (1981). Divided into three sections, the first section reviews the criticism, and problematises the novel in terms of history; the second section explores the portrayal of Indian history, and the third section examines the narrative technique employed in the novel.

I

Salman Rushdie's *Midnight's Children* is considered a trendsetter in Indian English novel both in terms of the themes and techniques. Winner of the Booker Prize in 1981 among the short listed novels: Salman Rushdie's *The Midnight's Children,* Molly Keane's *Good Behaviour,* Doris Lessing's *The Sirian Experiments,* Ian McEwan's *The Comfort of Strangers,* Ann Schlee's *Rhine Journey,* Muriel Spark's *Loitering with Intent,* D.M. Thomas's *The White Hotel. The Midnight Children* also won the Booker of the Booker in (1993) besides various other international prizes, the novel has been unparalleled in creating a history of sorts. *Midnight's Children* has been received not only as a work of startling originality but a landmark text in the genre of post-colonial fiction. The well known Indian novelist Anita Desai commented, in a book reading session, that she "was listening to the voice of a new age" (Desai vii).

Midnight's Children received overwhelming response from critics as well as the general readers. It should, however be noted that the appreciation of the novel is not entirely due to its intrinsic merit but also because of the style of narration. After the award of the Booker Prize to *Midnight's Children*, a critic notes with a hint of disapproval: "it was one of the few times in the recent history of British arts times in which it was an actual plus to have a funny foreign places" (Vorda 8). Aparna Mahanta reformulates the criticism in more extreme terms and argues that "Rushdie's novel did well in Britain because it was the latest in a long line of fictions to pander to western desires to see India as a strange sensual, tyrannical, fantastical other place" (Mahanta 244).

In the lack-luster world of post-war British fiction, Rushdie's exotic fantasies made a deep impact. The novel however has a lineage going back to Swift, Sterne, Waugh and Green: "Rushdie now steps into the gap, coming in the wake of the reigning nostalgia for the Raj, and decked with all the trappings of wit, humour and satire...Raj is not dead after all but lives on in the pseudo-sons, the Saleem Sinais" (Mahanta 244).

Rushdie also wrote on 'Raj revivalist' fictions and films in the United Kingdom. These fictions, Rushdie argues, are involved in "the creation of a false orient which, like mulligatawny soup, tries to taste Indian, but ends up being ultra parochially British, only with too much pepper" (Rushdie 88). Rushdie argues that political fictions 'revive the stereotypes of India inherited from the orientalist tradition. They make Indians bit-players in their own history, and they imply that the British, rather than the Indians, are "the ones whose stories matter" (Rushdie 90).

Primarily, Rushdie apprises that these fictions move forward a number of notions about history. Rushdie writes: "The view that the British and Indians actually understood each other jolly well...that the end of Empire was a sort of gentleman's agreement between old pals at the club...and, above all, the fantasy that the British Empire represented something 'noble' or 'great' about Britain" (Rushdie 101).

Interestingly, Rushdie's *Midnight's Children* represents not only an effect of the same 'Raj revival' but an antidote to it. The novel depicts India from an Indian point of view. It places Indians in the centre stage. *Midnight's Children* is successful in the West not because it resisted the 'Raj revival' but because it coincided with it. Mahanta argues that the novel draws substantially on European literary forms that cannot be said to be pitched at ordinary Indians but only at Westerners: "A tiny stratum of India's and Pakistan's elite, inheritors of the British mantle, the deracinated, speaking English, thinking English, dreaming English, Indians terrified, horrified, revolted by Indians and India, yet unable to escape the umbilical bonds" (Mahanta 244).

Mahanta traces out a problem with Rushdie's socio-cultural location. Subsequent critics foregrounded it too. Timothy Brennan, for instance, argues that "Rushdie cannot be said to speak from the perspective of, or on behalf of the 'Third World' citizens because his fiction is addressed primarily to a metropolitan intellectual elite" (Brennam 58). Similarly, Aijaz Ahmad and M. Keith Booker critique the stance of Rushdie: "Rushdie has been globally successful as a novelist because his privileged class location and his preference for sophisticated modernist and post-modernist narrative forms and ensures that his work conforms to the kinds of discourses authorised by the Anglo-American academy" (Ahmad 313).

Rushdie's fiction foregrounds the ambivalences of its own cultural location. Aijaz Ahmad argues: "there is a quality of linguistic quicksand in his writing that makes it seem as if he is a farmer...taking back with one hand what he has given with the other" (Ahmad 135). In similar lines, Tabish Khair argues that Rushdie's "self-criticism is a defensive maneuver that seeks to preempt criticism without providing enough space for the narration of the other whose criticism is being pre-empted" (Khair 297). It is Rushdie's capacity to 'stage' his marginality' knowingly for a mainstream audience while simultaneously mounting a critique of "the dominant political force of his writing" (Huggan 258).

Harish Trivedi is yet another critique, who is not impressed by the alleged subversiveness of Rushdie's language. He criticises Rushdie's claim that 'conquering' the English language through infiltration is a strategic step towards decolonisation. Trivedi observes that occasional sprinkling of Hindi-Urdu-Hindustani words and phrases in *Midnight's Children* does not change the basic ingredients of the English.

II

This section deals with the representation of history in Rushdie's *Midnight's Children.* Rushdie presents the post-Independence history in a critical manner. Written in three parts, the first part of the novel covers the period 1915-47, and is narrated in eight chapters. This part narrates the lives of the grandparents' generation, and establishes the trail of loss and disillusionment that begins with Aadam Aziz's loss of faith and his discovery of the God-shaped hole in his chest: "can't you see there's a hole in the middle of me the size of a melon?"(22).

The loss is association with knowledge whose outcome is division and doubts. Before his travel, the world is a paradise. This is a condition which transforms into loss of both innocence and belonging: "Now, returning he saw through travelled eyes...and felt sad, to be at home and feel so utterly enclosed" (11).

The novel begins with a sense of loss. Through the figure of Dr Aziz, the writer inaugurates the narrative of India's modernity as ambivalence and doubt. Aziz is aware that the treatment of his German friends is orientalist: "an invention of their ancestors' and was untrue, yet he was stranded in unbelief…unable to worship a God in whose existence he could not wholly disbelieve" (12).

The antithesis of Aadam Aziz's doubt is Tai, the boatman, a quirky enduring familiar spirit of the valley. His conviction of the continuity of existence is a kind of nihilistic. It recognises neither time nor the inevitability of change. It runs human history through the valley as if it were a personal spectacle. Tai refuses to wash because he deplores change, a characteristic fusion of the real and the metaphorical which is one of the methods of the novel.

The opening section also introduces the nose as an organ miracle. This is a misleading indicator of aristocratic ancestry. It is Tai, who first draws attention to the mystic powers of the nose: "A Nose like that, little idiot, is a great gift, I say: trust it" (17). Later the reader finds that Saleem Sinai's nose is miraculous.

Padma, the listener in the novel, appears in the opening section. She spends her days stirring vats of pickle. Padma, being Saleem's audience, is the unofficial listener. In Midnight's Children, the occupants of the magicians' quarter are representative of the people. Padma's earthiness is one of the many narrative expectations that Midnight's Children overturns. Padma's nobility lies in her uncomplicated directness, which is figured as a kind of integrity. Her tenderness affirms the unselfconscious truthfulness.

The central event of the first part is the extended courtship of Aziz and Naseem Ghani through the 'perforated sheet'. The early days of their marriage establishes their lifelong confrontation and the transformation of Naseem Aziz into the Reverend Mother: "A figure of melodramatic narrow-mindedness. The public narrative is that of approaching independence and the debate over partition. There is a dramatic account of the notorious Amritsar massacre" (36), where the British General Dyer ordered his soldiers to open fire on the civilian protesters. The event is representative of the decolonising process.

Another dimension of the independence narrative is the debate over Partition. This episode figures in the novel through Mian Abdullah, a Muslim. He opposes the Partition of India. His opposition is persuaded many other Muslims. The Muslims prefer the nation to religion. The Muslims include Aadam Aziz. Mian Abdullah is later recalled in the figure of Picture Singh, the most charming man in the world.

He presides over the magicians' quarter at the time of Indira Gandhi's emergency. He also speaks for India's multiplicity against the drive to simplify it. One of Mian Abdullah's followers is Nadir Khan the poet, who falls in love with Mumtaz, the daughter of Aadam Aziz and the mother of Saleem. The domestic narrative merges with the public one. This aspect is a characteristic conceit of the novel. The domestic aspect is taken at times to fantastic lengths.

The second part of the novel spans between 1947 and 1965. It tells of the birth of Saleem Sinai and of India. Pakistan was born the previous day. The narrator of the novel is absent from everything he earlier describes. This section has the story of the Methwold children. They are growing up and learn about their telepathic abilities. The narrative of childhood is intimate and painful.

Saleem suffers one facial humiliation after another culminating in the discovery of his miraculous powers while hiding in a washing basket full of dirty laundry. When the midnight's children are properly introduced, they signify a transforming potential of global magnitude: "As though history, arriving at a point of the highest significance and promise, had chosen to sow, in that instant, the seeds of a future which would genuinely differ from anything the world had seen up to that time" (195).

There were 1,001 children. Of them, 420 children die. The figure 420 is allusive to 'Shree 420,' a film. It has an important influence in Rushdie's work. It is as if the moment of India's independence is a moment of promise for humanity, signified by the 'Midnight's Children's Council as a group capable of profound understanding of each other. Corruption and cynicism could not allow the children to survive. Nehru's great ambition for post-independence India begins to disintegrate as soon as India is founded, in the partition violence and in the language marches. Throughout this period, Saleem's delusion grows.

In the middle of the novel, the suspicions about Saleem's parentage become evident to his father: "I should have known. Just look, where am I in that face. That nose, I should have" (236). Sinai thinks his wife had been unfaithful. Finally, the Sinai family moves to Pakistan. The move is a narrative of convoluted melodramas and lingering tragedies.

They return to Bombay during which Saleem's sinuses are drained and lost his miracle powers. Rushdie writes: "The operation whose ostensible purpose was the draining of my inflamed sinuses and the once-and-for-all clearing of my nasal passages had the effect of breaking whatever connection had been made in a washing-chest; of depriving me of nose-given telepathy" (304). There is another move to Pakistan. The section ends with the war between India and Pakistan in 1965. Saleem loses his memory as well as his home.

The third part of the novel, containing seven chapters, encompasses the period 1970-78. It recounts the events in East Pakistan. It leads to the breakup of Pakistan and the formation of Bangladesh. Saleem's nose has proved to have other miracle qualities. He can smell treachery, vengeance and mines. Saleem's nose is taken to East Pakistan, as 'a human dog' in a West Pakistani hit squad. The narrative gives about the killings in the Bangladesh war.

Saleem himself has no memory, no knowledge of himself, and brutalised by unselfconsciousness. He has no feelings. The miraculous is mundane. Saleem regains his memory in the Sundarbans. He is magically returned to Bombay by Parvati. One of the children of midnight is accompanied by Picture Singh. The novel ends with the defeat of Mrs Indira Gandhi. Timothy Brennan comments that the novel belongs to a genre of "the nationalism of Mourning" (Brennan 100).

Midnight's Children presents the new ideas of history. History is recorded by the techniques with which a period is evoked and involved. Avrom Freishman views: "What makes a historical novel historical is the active presence of a concept of history as a shaping force, and *Midnight's Children*...reflects awareness throughout that individual lives and national experiences are the products of material processes... shaped by history" (Fleishma 15).

According to Harry Shaw, "historical novels foreground history by representing historical milieu with a significant degree of probability". This is true of *Midnight's Children* since it foregrounds a sense of history. It also gives its locations like Bombay, Kashmir and Delhi sufficient "probability to allow readers to believe that historically real times and places are being described" (Shaw 20).

However, the probability of locations is not compromised by his simultaneous use of fabulism, anachronism and historical error. The criterion of probability does not mean straightforward "fidelity to the external world that a work represents; but can also depend upon how consistently a work follows its rules and patterns" (Shaw 21). *Midnight's Children* may be having purposeful mistakes of historical facts. This may be true in order to represent how an individual might have understood a viable historical moment.

The novel may have elements of fantasy. Fantasy however comments upon historically real situations, periods or places. *Midnight's Children* therefore remains historical because it is consistent to the criteria of historical veracity. In spite of lack of verisimilitude, *Midnight's Children* is concerned with history.

Rushdie narrates the subsequent events convincingly. Events pave the way to the simultaneous birth of the nation and its body in the form of Saleem between August 13 and 15. Other events include communal violence, Gandhi's peace march in Bengal, among others:

> ...a nation which had never previously existed was about to win its freedom, catapulting us into a world which, although it had five thousand years of history...was nevertheless quite imaginary, into a mythical land, a country which would never exist except...in a dream. (112)

And six hours before the midnight on August 15, William Methwold finally transfers his property to his Indian heirs and leaves the country. But he leaves his dishonesty behind in the womb of poor Vanitha. At the same hour, Amina goes into a 'prophecy-ridden' labour in a cabin of the Narlikar Nursing Home. Saleem's arrival into independent India coincides with Nehru's promise of a secular country. The hour of Independence is projected through celebrations and rituals in the streets and in Bombay. National tricolour flag is hoisted and Prime Minister Nehru makes his exuberant speech in the Assembly Hall in Delhi. In between these officially recorded events are the labour pains of expecting mothers, Partition riots, fires and the acts of violence.

The definitive version of the history of the Independence is replaced by the multiple vision of alternative reality. When the twin children were born, one to Amina the midwife Mary Pereira, the nurse changes the name tags of the babies giving the poor baby a life of privilege and condemning the rich-born child to poverty.

The protagonist, actually poor Vanitha's child in reality, was an Anglo-Indian, the illegitimate son of a departing coloniser and a poor Hindu woman. Saleem represents the newly born post-colonial nation state. The post-colonial children are no longer to do with the concept of origin or purity. Time is hybrid and so is history. There are lines in the movement of time and of history. When the Sinais eventually discover the betrayal of Mary Pereira, they reconcile themselves to the fact of Saleem's miscegenation: "We all found that it made no difference! I was still their son: they remained my parents. In a kind of collective failure of imagination we learned that we simply could not think our way out of our pasts" (118).

As far as the historical aspects are concerned, the novel depicts the events and experiences in the lives of three generations of the Sinai family. *Midnight's Children* seeks to explore three aspects: the commingling of autobiography and narrative; the breach of chronology; and the search for identity and the meaning of life. The opening of the novel explains these aspects: "I was born in the city of Bombay…once upon a time, No that won't do there's no getting away from the date: I was born in Dr Narlikar's Nursing Home on August 15, 1947. And the time? On the stroke of midnight, as a matter of fact…I had been mysteriously handcuffed to history" (1-2).

The first sentence of the novel is illustrative of the hybrid art. The tale is meant to be an autobiography and a narrative. It is an account of facts and a yarn spurn out of imagination. It is a blend of truth and fiction clearly setting the tone for an autobiography. The novelist gives least priority with regard to the observance of chronology. There is a frequent forward or backward shift in time.

The title of the novel is connotatively historical. The midnight is a point where the past and the future amalgamate into the present. The midnight of 14-15 August, 1947 sees the birth of the narrator and the country making new avenues of hope. Saleem is Rushdie's fictional ego. He is an allegorical representation of India.

Rushdie seems to be offering a subaltern solution to India's many problems, by concluding the novel with its focus on the boy and his failure. Saleem is tempted to fill in the jar of the future too "One empty jar…how to end?"(461), but resists doing. Though he writes *his* own future, he does not touch the jar. "But the future cannot be a reserved jar; one jar must remain empty" (462).

Saleem's narration of Indian history then is alternative history, a tale of the marginalised under history, and an assertion of his polyglot identity as an Indian. Rushdie ignores the concept of historical truth as a recorded fact. Hutcheon defines this process as the "textual self awareness" that pervades metafiction, or "fiction that includes within itself commentary on its own narrative and or linguistic identity" (Hutcheon 1).

The imaginary truth is conveyed through a complex strategy. The centre of the narrative is the narrator-protagonist Saleem Sinai. He is emblematic of a supreme moment of history, a crystallisation of an evolving mood, a distillation of a vision, nostalgic, critical and philosophical. But in spite of it, he is able to project what may be called a sort of prismatic vision of reality, partial, fissured and fragmented, but highly absorbing and deeply meaningful. Afraid of absurdity, "he is frantically engaged in a quest for meaning" (4).

In the post-modern literary tradition, an absence of universal truth replaces prior notions of one absolute truth in terms of history. Just as post-modernism dismantles the concept of absolute truth, Rushdie's novel dismantles the notion of official version of history.

III

The novel offers innovative narrative techniques. He sets the trend of experimentation with narrative technique and the English language. He gives the genre of Indian English fiction a new direction. The complexity of his narrative technique is what really attracts the attention of the readers and critics: "Combining the elements of magic and fantasy, the grimmest realism, extravagant farce, multi-mirrored analogy and a potent symbolic structure, Salman Rushdie has captured the astonishing energy of the novel unprecedented in scope" (Wash 257).

Rushdie's objective in the novel has been to create awareness about the world of magic, which defies logic and realistic narrative. However, the narrative style of *Midnight's Children* is accessible to the readers. Rushdie drops the idea of the linear narrative and the omniscient author tradition as he offers a detailed description of seventy-five years of the subcontinent's history. The narrative style of *Midnight's Children*, argues Banerjee, "cannot be separated.

In fact, it can be read as a political history rather than a fantasy. The critics read the text as a non-fiction and also as a political allegory" (Banerjee 198).

There are two intertwined narrative streams in the novel. First, Saleem's account of his own life starting from his grandparents, the personal line of action or the fictional narrative. Second, the public line of action or historical narrative giving an account of the historical events that inform the collective experience of the people. The personal line entrances the confessional or autobiographical strain through memory. In an attempt to give the meaning of his life, Saleem explores the meaning of life in a historical mode so that the novel is about the protagonist as well as about contemporary India and the meaning of Indian Independence.

William Walsh points out that the purpose of Rushdie's *Midnight's Children* is "the personification and realisation of Indian life" (Walsh 257). The novel is about a person who was born in India but settled abroad. He tries to recreate his homeland, mixing memory and desire, fact and fantasy, reality and vision, time and timelessness. Rushdie suggestively remarks: "And one such suspicious generalisation may be that writers in my position, exiles or emigrants or expatriates, are haunted by some sense of loss, some urge to reclaim, to look back, even at the risk of being mutated into pillars of salt. But if we do look back" (Rushdie 5).

Linda Hutcheon's concept of the "Narcissistic narrative" exemplifies the post-modernist undermining of official version of history: "The origins of the self-reflecting structure that governs many modern novels might well lie in that parodic intent basic to the genre as it began in *Don Quixote*" (Hutcheon 18). Rushdie's narrative is suggestive of a narratorial awareness. It invites the reader to participate in questioning the accepted version of history. Hutcheon argues that "what narcissistic narrative does in flaunting, in baring its fictional and linguistic systems to the reader's view is to transform the *process* that is explicitly called into action, in both the author and the reader" (Hutcheon 20).

Rushdie's novel instead emphasises the creative process. The narrator breaks down old conventions and proposes replacements.

Rushdie writes when new theories of history undermine recorded historical facts. *Midnight's Children* provides the means of looking at older historical forms. It provides an example that explores new views of history.

Saleem Sinai, the narrator welcomes the serious reader to involve in creating and discovering an alternative to what is accepted. He depends on memory and the process of recalling memories. This technique embraces the individual histories that overlap some aspects of recorded history.

There are two aspects of Rushdie's narrative. The first one is the self-aware narratorial style; and the second one is the participation of the reader. Through this strategy of narrative, Rushdie undermines the conventional ideas of history and posits a multiplicity of histories. The narrative provides a chutnified mixture of memory and recorded fact.

Rushdie's undermining of absolute historical truth as a recorded fact gives credence to what he writes. The otherwise self-conscious narration is more internalised and structural. Saleem's narration in *Midnight's Children* is overt. Hutcheon defines it: "texts in which the self-consciousness and self reflection are clearly evident, usually explicitly thematised or even allegorised within the 'fiction'," (Hutcheon 20).

Saleem draws attention to the act of writing. He informs the reader of his self-aware narrative state. Saleem uses Padma as a tool to communicate this awareness to the audience: "Padma has started getting irritated whenever my narration becomes self-conscious, whenever, like an incompetent puppeteer; I reveal the hands holding the strings" (72). Saleem demonstrates the awareness of his narrative.

The self-conscious narrative extends through the fictive world created by Rushdie. The narrative relies upon the reader to participate in the creation of meaning: "This productive labour is no longer the explicit subject of overt teachings to the reader, the text now forces him to read with his imaginative and ordering faculties alert and at work" (Hutcheon 20). The self-conscious narrative in turn engages the reader on the level of plot and story. It forces the reader to delve beyond the surface of the text. Thus, the narrative helps the author in discovering alternative meanings. Hutcheon writes: "For Rushdie, there is no question about intended reader participation: Saleem's invitation to the reader lacks subtly. He directly affirms that he expects "my audience to be capable of joining in; of imagining" (Hutcheon 82).

Rushdie uses Saleem to implore the reader to accept an alternative to traditional notions of history. It entreats the reader to explore the alternatives. The narrative of self-awareness may indulge in intentional errors in the text. The errors instigate the reader to situate the error in the realm of a reality. Rushdie explains:

> Reality is a question of perspective. Re-reading my work, I have discovered an error in chronology. The assassination of Mahatma Gandhi, in these pages, on the wrong date. But I cannot say, now, what the actual sequence of events might have been; in my India, Gandhi will continue to die at the wrong time. Does one error invalidate the entire fabric...? Today, in my confusion, I can't judge. I'll have to leave it to others. (198)

Saleem refers to such events as Gandhi's death regardless of what is recorded as fact. Rushdie's participative narration enables new approaches to history. Memory becomes a viable historical alternative to recorded fact. Michael Reder observes: "when Rushdie speaks of 'memory,' he is speaking not of cultural memory or national consciousness but of individual: it is not the dominant, official *History* but a history that is personalised and therefore given life, significance, and meaning" (Reder 225).

The narrator-protagonist is an indifferent character. He is preoccupied with omniscience. Multiplicity of events attempt to weave into his life as well as his narrative: "If I seem a little bizarre, remember the wild profession of my inheritance...perhaps if one wishes to remain an individual in the midst of the teeming multitudes, one must make oneself grotesque" (109). The female character Padma is satisfied as she understands that at last Saleem learns how to tell things really fast.

Rushdie makes free use of fantasy and willful anachronism. There are revealing structural similarities between the two fictions.

Saleem entertains the readers with a great deal of fun through his fascinating story.

Rushdie's contribution to the new Indian English novel lies in his experiments with English language. Rushdie however was new to experiments with English. Raja Rao was the first to experiment with new narrative techniques in *Kanthapura* (1938). He applies the grandmother as a narrator.

Kamala Markandaya uses similar technique in her *Nectar in a Sieve* (1954) where the narrator is again a grandmother. R.K. Narayan adopts a flashback technique in *The Guide* (1958). The point of view technique or multiple narrators is used first by Chaman Nahal in *Azadi* (1975). Rushdie's narrative technique in *Midnight's Children* (1981) is beyond the experiments in the past.

Works Cited

Ahmad, Aizaz and Booker, M. Keith. "*Midnight's Children* in History and Complexity: Reading Rushdie after the cold war." *Critical Essays on Salman Rushdie.* Ed. M. Keith Booker. New York: G. K. Hall, 1999. Print.

Ahmad, Aijaz. *In Theory: Classes, Nations, Literatures.* London: Verso, 1992. Print.

Brennan, Timothy. *Salman Rushdie and the Third World.* London: Macmillan, 1989. Print.

—. *Salman Rushdie and the third World: Myths of the Nation Basingstoke.* London: Macmillan, 1989. Print.

Banerjee, Ashutosh. "Narrative Technique in *Midnight's Children.*" *Three Contemporary Novelists.* Ed. Dr R.K. Dhawan. Prestige Publication, Delhi: 1985. Print.

Desai, Anita. 'Introduction' in Salman Rushdie's *Midnight's Children.* London: Everyman, 1995. Print.

Fleishman, Avrom. *The English Historical Novel: Walter Scott to Virginia Woolf.* Baltimore: Johns Hopkins, 1971. Print.

Harry, Shaw. *The Forms of Historical Fiction: Sir Walter Scott and His Successors.* Ithaca: CUP, 1983. Print.

—. *The Forms of Historical Fiction: Sir Walter Scott and His Successors.* Ithaca: CUP, 1983.Print.

Huggan, Graham. *The Post-Colonial Exotic: Marketing and Margins.* London: Routledge, 2001. Print.

—. *The Post-Colonial Exotic: Marketing and Margins.* London: Routledge, 2001. Print.

—. *The Post-Colonial Exotic: Marketing and Margins.* London: Routledge, 2001. Print.

Hutcheon, Linda. *Narcissistic Narrative: The Metafictional Paradox.* Waterloo: Wilfred Laurier UP, 1980. Print.

—. *A Poetics of Postmodernism: History, Theory, Fiction.* New York: Routledge, 1988. Print.

—. *A Poetics of Postmodernism: History, Theory, Fiction.* New York: Routledge, 1988. Print.

—. *A Poetics of Postmodernism: History, Theory, Fiction.* New York: Routledge, 1988. Print.

—. *A Poetics of Postmodernism: History, Theory, Fiction.* New York: Routledge, 1988. Print.

Khair, Tabish. *Babu Fictions: Alienation in Contemporary Indian English Novels.* New Delhi: Oxford UP, 2001. Print.

Mahanta, Aparna. "Allegories of the Indian Experience: The Novels of Salman Rushdie." *Economic and Political Weekly* 19.6 (1984).Print.

—. "Allegories of the Indian Experience: The Novels of Salman Rushdie." *Economic and Political Weekly* 19.6 (1984). Print.

—. "Allegories of the Indian Experience: the Novels of Salman Rushdie." *Economic and Political Weekly* 19.6 (1984). Print.

Michael, Reder. "Rewriting History and Identity: The Reinvention of Myth, Epic, and Allegory in Salman Rushdie's *Midnight's Children.*" *Critical Essays on Salman Rushdie.* Ed. M. Keith Booker. NewYork: G.K. Hall and Co, 1999. Print.

Rushdie, Salman. *The Imaginary Homeland: Essays and Criticism: 1981*-1991. London: Granta, 1991. Print.

—. *The Imaginary Home Land: Essays and Criticism: 1981*- 1991. London: Granta, 1991. Print.

—. *The Imaginary Home Land: Essays and Criticism: 1981*- 1991. London: Granta, 1991. Print.

Rushdie, Salman. *The Midnight's Children.* New York: Avon Books, 1982. (All the parentheses quotes are taken from the text.)

Rushdie, Salman. "Reclaiming a City and a History." *Express Magazine and The Indian Express* March 11, 1984. Print.

Vorda, Allan. 'Stuck on the Margins: An Interview with Kazuo Ishiguro' in *Face to Face: Interviews with Contemporary Novelists.* Houston: Rice University Press, 1993. Print.

Walsh, William. *India and the Novel: The New Pelican Guide to English Literature.* Vol. 7. Harmondsworth: Penguin Books, 1983. Print.

—. *India and the Novel: The New Pelican Guide to English Literature.* Vol. 8. Harmondsworth: Penguin Books, 1983. Print.

Chapter - 5

'Death More Profitable than Life': A Critique of Caste, Patriarchcy, Communism in *The God of Small Things*

This chapter examines Arundhati Roy's *The God of Small Things* (1997) with a focus on the portrayal of caste, patriarchy and communism as portrayed in the novel. Divided into four sections, the first section of the chapter explores the contextualisation of the novel; the second section examines the question of caste; the third section discusses the critique of patriarchy; and the fourth section delineates the criticism of communism. It is argued by the end of the chapter that Roy is very critical of the institutions of caste, patriarchy and communism, which have a decisive bearing impeding the modernisation of India.

I

With the publication of Arundhati Roy's *The God of Small Things*, the Indian novel in English received yet another jolt in the publishing market and critical enterprise. The awarding of Man Booker Prize to *The God of Small Things* in 1997 generated debate about the genre. Having been selected for the Booker among the short list that include Jim Crace's *Quarantine,* Mick Jackson's *The Underground Man,* Bernard Mac Laverty's *Grace Notes,* Tim Parks's *Europa*, Madeleine's *St John's The Essence of the Thing*, *The God of Small Things* became a forerunner of a new aspect of writing the local. The Chairperson of the jury, Gillian Beer remarks: "With extraordinary linguistic inventiveness, Arundhati Roy funnels the history of South India through the eyes of seven-years-old twins. The story she tells is fundamental as well as local...Her narrative crackles with riddles and yet tells its tale quite clearly" (Beer 12).

One of the most written about novels, *The God of Small Things* is interpreted in varied ways from the perspectives of caste, religion, gender, among others. R. S. Sharma and Shashibala Talwar view that the multiplicity of approaches will seem counter to the idea of a unifying theme:

> The proper reading strategy requires an assumption that the novel has single theme and that the other concerns...are subordinate to the central argument or vision. This procedure will facilitate analysis as well as evaluation of their novel as a unified product of creative writing (Sharma 42-43).

Some *critics* sought to interpret the book that they can look for the controlling or key metaphor of the novel in its title, for it is likely to give a clue to the novel. *The God of Small Things* is about the life of the weak and the helpless. There may be small creatures like blue bottles, frogs and ants or human beings such as the victims of Hollick's lust or the factory worker-woman who supplies Chacko's needs or children like Estha and Rahel who are victims of orange-drink-lemon-drink man or Baby Kochamma or the downtrodden like Vellya Papapen and his sons Velutha and Kuttapen or the ostracized ones like Ammu. *The God of Small Things* represents all these people who are victimised by the forces of history, convention, false pride and respectability, the tyranny of the state and the simple natural life of children.

With the publication of *The God of Small Things* and because of her activism, Roy became a popular personality. Having been sold more than six million copies in forty languages, the novel made the author world famous. The novel, which took four and a half years to be written, received an overwhelming response with raving reviews across the world.

The novel is about Ammu, the divorced daughter of the Ayemenem House and her children Estha and Rahel. Ammu's relationship with the untouchable Velutha turns tragic in quick succession creating uproar coupled with the death of Sophie-Mol, the cousin of the twins. Velutha dies in police custody leading to the tragic separation of Ammu and her children.

The Ayemenem house has living in it all people cursed and they suffer either because of transgression or betrayal. After retiring, Pappachi leads a lonely life with Mammachi venturing into the establishment of a pickle and Jam factory. Chacko, their son tries to keep the factory going. Baby Kochamma, Chacko's sister tries to seduce an English priest and when she fails, she returns to Ayemenem House. Chacko magnanimously invites his divorced wife and daughter Sophie for the holidays when Margaret's English husband dies in an accident.

Ammu, Chacko's sister, and the mother of the twins, runs away from her alcoholic husband, a Bengali and comes back to his house in Ayemenem with the twin children. But her family develops hatred towards her and made her live lonely from the society. Over a period of time, the alienated life of Ammu leads to liaison with Velutha who belongs to a dalit community.

Roy's fame has not been like a flash in the pan. She is more than an exotic literary figure in the Indian writing in English. When the nation celebrated its nuclear tests in 1998, Roy wrote a critique criticising the nuclear policy. She is known for organising massive protest marches against construction of a dam on the Narmada River which results in submerging of around 245 villages in Gujarat state. It is her strong social and political consciousness and the irrepressible rebellious spirit that causes the novelist seeking justice for the people. Ganapathi Reddy writes about her social stance: "Unlike many other Indian authors of international fame, she has been focusing her attention on issues of livelihood in the world's largest democracy by pursuing more direct and participative approaches towards public mobilisation through social and mass movements method, giving voice to voiceless (Reddy 16).

While the leading writers and artists are preoccupied with the intellectual interests and isolation, Roy exhibited concern for the masses. She is actively involved in upholding the cause of the marginalised sections of the Indian society with her passionate sense of justice. Harriet Gilbert in this regard opines: "Arundhati Roy is a high profile celebrity certain sections of media instinctively sympathise with her cause. And the general feeling is the big dams destroy communities forcibly, which are misguided. And also affecting the wild life" (Reddy 16).

Roy's highly critical essay "the Greater Common Good" written after her stay at the construction of the Sardar Sarovar dam on the Naramada disillusioned the Supreme Court to the extent that a justice remarked that Roy had undermined the dignity of the court and sought action against her. She was even made to go through a day's symbolic imprisonment. Yet she continued to work for the cause of the people. Her critics blame her of using her celebrity. Roy believes that she is letting her fame use her. There is criticism that since she belongs to the urban elite family, she cannot comment on rural problems, she replies that it is a serious responsibility of the urban elite to support the protest that is started by the powerless people in the village because these underclass people are victimized by the state and the press.

Arundhati Roy brings the same kind of passion to the treatment of *The God of Small Things*. Critics compared her writing with William Faulker, Gabriel Marquez and Salman Rushdie.The greatness of Arundhati Roy's activism results in the fact that she has been an active participant in the socio-environmental issues. She has become popular for writing public causes in fighting for the justice. This novel however has become so popular that the highest sale of the book after its release stood at a whopping 3.5 lakh copies.

True to what D. H. Laurence once said: "All creative art must arise out of a specific soil and flickers with a spirit of place: (Mc Donald 334), *The God of Small Things* was imagined on a vast canvas of her memory, most of which can be traced out to her childhood in a Kerala Village. Throughout the novel, Kerala remains a vibrant, throbbing presence. The reader is never allowed to forget that one is in god's own country, whether it is in the exquisitely drawn picture of the landscape or in the description of the attitudes, morals and mores of the people there or in projecting the blatantly hypocritical behaviour of the people in power or in the state's machinery. The novel received an overwhelming response from a cross-section of readers and critics.

Dhawan writes on the success of Roy: "She is young, charming, rich and famous. She is the writer of the mega wonder novel, *The God of Small Things*. A writer whose novel is authentically Indian as is her writing style. One who has put India on the map of the English speaking world?" (Dhawan 21-22).

Having some autobiographical elements, *The God of Small Things* chronicles the lives of Syrian orthodox Christian family in Kerala. Roy admits: in some ways small things is a story that has always been with me. She confesses in an interview:

> Fiction for me has been a way of trying to make sense of the world as I know it. It is located very close to me the book. It is located in the village. I grew up in, if I had to put it very simply, it is about trying to make the connections between the smallest of things and the biggest ones. (Speath 4)

The novel with autobiographical overtones describes the family occupying Ayemenem house. By virtue of a keener sensibility and subjective experience, Roy is able to perceive the subversive impact on the colonisation. Roy views that the book is the experience of thirty seven years of her life, her own fears with which anyone would agree or disagree with. She observes: "for me the book is not about what happened, but about how what happened affected people" (Wilber 46).

The novel is basically about despair, emptiness and failure, characteristic of an ex-colonial society. Set in Kerala in the 1960s in the throes of the Communist rule, the novel focuses on the inevitable and drastic consequences of the situation on the personal lives of the members of a Syrian Christian family and the Dalit community. The book explicitly demonstrates how even in the days of decolonisation the racial discriminations and political exploitations persist resulting in violent repercussions on private lives. Roy brings out the ex-colonial society's inability to make a complete break from its colonial past and fight against the forces. In the very beginning of the novel, the novelist explores the lush green post-monsoon scene that:

> But by early June the south-west monsoon breaks: the country side turns a commodest green. Boundaries blur as tapioca fences

> take root and bloom. Brick walls turn moss green. Pepper wines snake up electric poles. Wild creepers burst through laterite banks and spill across the flooded roads. Boats ply in the bazaars. And small fish appear in the puddles that fill the PWD potholes on the highways. (1)

The monsoon in Kerala is riveting because of the vegetation of the region, the captivating landscape, which is adjacent to Arabian Sea. The Meenachal River flows through the Kottayam district which has a large Christian population. The landscape and the river do not end up merely providing a backdrop to the novel but become an integral part of the novel. The Meenachal River which makes such things happen in a day that it changes the lives of Rahel, Estha, Ammu and Velutha forever. In respect of the landscape, Roy seems to agree with Chekov, who writes: "In descriptions of nature one has to snatch at small detail, grouping them in such a manner that after reading them one can obtain the picture on closing one's eyes" (Chekov 5).

II

This section examines the question of caste with a focus on the aspect of the suppression of untouchables, whose life is conditioned in all realms of life due to callous attitude of the upper caste people. It also examines how the politics is practiced against the common people in order to thwart the progression of Dalits in the Ayemenem society. Roy strongly opposes the dreadful aspects meted out to the Dalits in the name of caste. Particularly, the Paravan community people experienced terrible life in all social contexts. It portrays how the main character Velutha is killed since he belongs to one of the untouchable castes, Paravan. The Dalits lead a miserable life.

Narayan, a Dalit character in Rohinton Mistry's *A Fine Balance* puts it aptly: "More than twenty years have passed since independence. How much longer? I want to be able to drink from the village well, worship in the temple, walk where I like" (Mistry 142). The practice of untouchability, supported by religion, seems to be a prominent theme in the novel. The casteism continued for thousands of years: "A feeling which refuses to accept the fact that the untouchable is a human being, but insists on treating him like a subhuman creature to be ignored or bellied or exploited as occasion demands" (Naik 29). Another critic, Cowasjee explains how the Hindu religion perpetrated the caste system: "Hindu religion is responsible for this fiendish segregation of humanity: the waste products of the body are unclean, therefore, those who carry them are dirty and obnoxious" (Cowasjee 51). Balaram Gupta opines in this regard: "The condition of the untouchable in India in the pre-independence past was no different from that of the American Negro, since he was subjected to the same kind of typification that his American counterpart had to suffer for centuries a typification that spelt deprivation, exploitation" (Gupta 13).

Roy talks about the sad plight of the untouchables *Paravan* in the most authentic and graphic detail and historical manner. Roy writes: "When the British came to Malabar, a number of *Paravans*, *Pelayas* and *Pulayas* (among them Velutha's grandfather, Kelan were converted to Christianity and joined the Anglican Church to escape the scourge of untouchability. As added incentive they were given a little food and money. They were known as Rice-Christians" (74).

The religion sanctifies and perpetuates untouchability among caste-Hindus and caste-Christians. The Christian family is headed by Mammachi in which she takes pride in its lineage and heritage with people like Punnyan Kunju being legends of that region. The spread of Christianity has not resulted in undermining the hold of Hinduism. Hence Christianity sustained some of the worst practices of Hinduism like untouchability.

Many of the Paravans and Pulayans got converted to Christianity to escape the scourge of untouchability. But the conversion made hardly any change in the lives of the Dalits. Roy writes:

> It didn't take them long to realise that they had jumped from the frying pan into the fire. They were made to have separate churches, with separate services, and separate priests. As a special favour they were even given their own separate Pariah Bishop. After independence they found they were not entitled to any government benefits like job reservations or bank loans at low interest rates, because officially, on paper, they were Christians, and therefore casteless. (74)

The Dalit Christians are deprived of the privileges available to the untouchables among Hindus. The caste consciousness among the Christians makes Kochu Maria wear Kunuku because otherwise "how would people know that despite her lowly cook's job she was a Syrian Christian, Mar Thomite? Not a Pelaya or a Pulaya or a Paravan. But a Touchable upper caste Christian" (170).

Syrian Christians are intolerable to the poor untouchables. The upper caste Syrian Christians are no better than the caste-Hindus in practicing untouchability and inflicting boundless harm to the Dalits. Mammachi tells Estha and Rahel: "Caste Hindus and caste Christians Mammachi told Estha and Rahel that she could remember a time, in her girlhood, when *Paravan's* footprint. In Mammachi's time, *Paravans,* like other Untouchables, were not allowed to walk on public roads..." (73).

They are not allowed to wrap their upper bodies and not allowed to carry umbrellas. His father Vellya Paapen who has seen the days of "crawling backwards" to remove pollution of touch has reconciled to his present state and even feels that Mammachi and her family are generous and helpful: "Mammachi remembered a time in her girlhood. When Paravans were expected to crawl backwards with a broom sweeping away the footprints so that, Brahims or Syrian Christians would not defile themselves by accidently stepping into a Paravans footprint" (74).

Velutha becomes a member of the Communist party in Kerala. He acquires social awareness in his profession by moving around places where people are better placed than his community people. As a result, he became a follower of Communist philosophy. Velutha's morality and self-esteem is intimidated by his employees and is feared by his father. The upper caste people are surprised to see Velutha's behaviour when it does not comply with their expectations like his brother Kuttapans. For instance, Baby Kochamma describes to the Inspector Thomas Mathew "...It was not just *what* Velutha had said that made her come to the police, but the way he said it" (260).

Vellya Paapen, Velutha's father also realises the predicament of the untouchables. He fails to understand the significance of Velutha's exceeding his traditional caste occupation of coconut tree climbing. Vellya Paapen as a father would fear any deviant behaviour from the accepted norms of society. Vellya Paapen and Velutha represent two generations of untouchables. Vellya Paapen complies with the existing norms of society. Velutha represents the self-confident, experienced assertive young generation of the Dalits.

Velutha struggles hard to get the social acceptance and recognition. He dares to fall in love with Ammu, an upper caste woman. Ultimately he pays a heavy price. His party, which he hopes to support him, declares that the party would not be supporting such heinous aspects. In this regard, Darshana Trivedi writes: "The novel is about the novelist's personal sufferings, her own experiences while living with social realities of Kerala...The difference between Anand and Roy is that Anand observes outwardly, while Roy suffers inwardly" (Trivedi 188).

Being inexperienced, Velutha is unable to understand the ridiculous rules. Velutha does not understand the undercurrents of the discrimination. Though he attempts to defend himself, he is beaten to death by Inspector Mathew in Police lockup. "There is no virtue in the global laundry lists with woman as a pious item. Representation has not withered away. The female intellectual has a circumscribed task which she must not disown with a flourish" (Spivak 308).

Spivak commends the responsibility on the part of the intellectual class to represent the subaltern by raising their voices. This change can only be brought about by an insurgency that is why Roy remarks that "things can change in a day" (202). She makes the readers aware that the world can be changed in a day, but it needs a revolution: "Revolution is not a dinner party. Revolution is an insurrection, an act of violence, in which one class overthrows another" (280).

Roy draws the attention of the readers to adopt the innocence of the twins—Estha and Rahel, who in spite of living in India, do not have awareness of their caste, religion and boundaries. They are deeply unaware of this cruel world. Linda Duits writes: "I had this thing that I think Pink also had: like, look, I can do what I want and if you don't want me like that, well, that's your loss. I have this thing like: yeah, if you don't like me, you don't like me. That's something I didn't have before" (Duits 41).

The Booker jury describes the novel as dealing with 'love and death,' which is because of the caste system. The attack is not based on witnessed truth but on a fictive creation of homogenous society where the upper caste people suppress the lower caste people. The narrative reveals an inaccurate repression of intra-caste relations.

Jason Cowley, one of the five Booker Judges, explains: "Why we Chose Arundhati, writes "Roy's achievement is never to forget about small things in life, the insects and flowers, wind and water, the outcaste and despised" (Cowley 28). Roy shows in the novel the paradoxes inherent in the Indian social and political set up, and relates the plight of the downtrodden to these tendencies.

III

This section examines Roy's portrayal of women's struggle to free from the patriarchal society. She critiques the Indian way of life in which the women are conditioned to follow the patriarchal norms. The discrimination of women is one of the major themes in the novel. The novel encompasses such aspects as love and hate, love and sex, marriage and divorce, conflict and struggle and above all it is about women. It shows the conflict between men and women. Abraham writes in this regard: "Respectable Syrian Christians must feel that the book, however, maligns the community and particularly its womanhood. The explicit reference to sex is bad enough but a Syrian Christian woman would make love to an untouchable youth is clearly obscene" (Abraham 3).

The relationship between Ammu and Velutha and that of Estha and Rahel have elements of obscenity and vulgarity. Roy's treatment of sexuality is considered an imitation of Euro-American fiction. The treatment of sexual experience and increasing frankness about normal and abnormal sex are presented as the final realm of both pleasure and truth. Ahmed writes in this connection: "as in the western counterparts, in Roy's novel, phallocentricity operates to dismiss the actually constituted field of politics and either irrelevant or a zone of bad faith" (Ahmed 103).

Baby Kochamma and Mammachi belong to the third generation. Baby Kochamma falls in love with a handsome young Irish monk, father Mulligan when she was eighteen. The young girl and the intrepid Jesuit are carried away by passion. She joins the convent in Madras after becoming a Roman Catholic with special permission from the Vatican. She hopes that it would provide her opportunities to be with father Mulligan. The love affair however did not materialise. She was subsequently sent abroad for studies. She returns with a diploma in ornamental Gardening. After fifty years, she abandons gardening and falls in love with dish antennae.

Ammu is found to be in the clutches of patriarchal society. Her father always beats her mother with brass vase. Once the mother and the daughter are thrown out of the house. She is denied higher education due to her father's callous attitude. He thinks that higher education damages the life of a female child. He also considers that girls do not need education. Ammu's brother, on the other hand, is sent for higher education. It is clearly shown in the novel that there is a gender prejudice and discrimination in the family between a male and a female child. Since she is neglected, she wishes to marry anybody during her short visit to Calcutta: "She thought anyone at all would be better, than returning to Ayemenom" (39).

But the person to whom she gets married is an alcoholic who asks her to sleep with Mr Hollick, who is her husband's boss on a tea estate in Assam. She objects to this proposal and finally hits her husband with a heavy book and leaves the place. When she comes back to her village with her twins to live in her parents' house, she is unwelcome. Again her brother has been given importance in her parental house. He becomes the owner of the parental property.

Ammu's life is an example of struggle for livelihood. Sharma remarks in this connection: "Her death in ignominy, and disgraceful cremation bring the story of her life to an end-more sinned against than sinning" (Sharma 78). In spite of all the troubles, she gives importance to the love and care of the twins. Once, the family members attend the funeral ceremony of Sophie Mol. She is married to a Bengali Hindu without her parents' consent. Therefore she is not allowed to go closer to other family members.

She is accused of having sexual relationship with Velutha, a low caste person. When she goes to police station, her statement is not recorded. Besides, she is treated badly by inspector Thomas Mathew. Roy writes: "He starred at Ammu's breast as she spoke. He said the police knew all they needed to know and that the Kottayam police didn't take statements from Veshya or their illegitimate children. Ammu said she'd see about that. Inspector Thomas came around his desk baton. If I were you,' he said, I'd go home quietly" (8).

The novelist's depiction of Ammu's identity is suggestive that she has no identity as a woman. Ammu's episode is an instance of atrocities and ill-treatment of a woman by the police. The police Inspector calls her a '*veshya*,' prostitute. Her platonic relationship with Velutha is a realisation that even the small things matter in one's life.

The death of Velutha is reported as natural. Roy's portrayal of the relationship between Ammu and Velutha is unacceptable to the caste-ridden patriarchal society. Ammu's material life like many Indian women signifies a heterogeneous relationship between a wife and a husband. She craves for escaping from the realm of marital relationship. She leaves her husband and comes back to her parental village.

Her marriage itself may be understood as an escape from her family and village. She does not ponder much when she took her decision of marriage. Roy describes: "The proposal of Ammu, five days after they first met Ammu didn't pretend to be in love with him. She just weighed the odds and accepted. She thought that anything, anyone at all would be better than returning to Ayemenem" (39).

Roy showcases how the Indian women have no liberty, freedom and autonomy in Ayemenem society. Male dominance is visible in Pappachi-Mammachi family. The familial relationship is devoid of love. Ammu, Pappachi's daughter is reminded of her childhood days in Delhi, where her Entomologist father used to act like bully. Roy writes: "He donated money to orphanage and leprosy clinics. He worked hard on his public profile as a sophisticated, generous, moral man but alone with his wife and children he turned into a monstrous suspicious bully, with a streak of vicious cunning" (180).

Because of his male ego, Pappachi tortures his wife and children. He is "not content with having beaten up his wife and daughter he tore down curtains, kicked furniture and smashed a table lamp" (181). Their relationship is filled with jealously, violence and hatred. Pappachi is envious of the pickle factory of his wife. Mammachi's life seems to be sandwiched between the cruelties of her husband and her own responsibilities. The female characters fail to cope with the situation. There is a gender bias in Mammachi's treatment of his daughter Ammu and her son Chacko who becomes the inheritor of all her property.

Chacko married an English woman, Margaret, who later on divorced him and married Joe. Their daughter Sophie Mol dies by drowning herself. The divorce signifies the changing traditional familial structure of the Indian in society, which is in contact with the Western culture. Simone de Beauvoir writes: "Woman herself recognises that the world is masculine on the whole; those who fashioned it, ruled it, and still dominate it today are men. As for her, she does not consider herself responsible for it; it is understood that she is inferior and dependent" (Beauvoir 609).

Rahel, Ammu's daughter, who is mischievous, is expelled for her cantankerous behaviour. Her smoking too is not acceptable. Being slow in studies, she takes eight years to complete five years course in a mediocre college of architecture. Rahel is bold enough to face problems. Having entered into the contact with Larry Mc Caslin, they fall in love leading to marriage: "She drifted into marriage like a passenger drifts towards an unoccupied chair in an airport lounge with a Sitting Down sense" (18). Though accompanied her husband to America, she soon realises the greatness of Indian culture. The self-introspection looms over her desires and keeps her away from that pleasure.

Being unable to understand the reason behind, she gets bewildered: "it was always in the colours of the dark, oiled wood of boat and empty cores of the tongues of flame that flickered in brass lamp" (73). Probably her longing for marital pleasures takes her to the land of hollowness. She finds absurdity in her married life and seeks divorce. She is a symbol of true Indian immigrant experience.

Her body is Western while her spirit Indian. Kulkarni views: "probably with lost hopes and unsatisfied desires, Rahel represents the contemporary women representing the Western land-culturally barren, morally empty and socially inimical (Kulakarni 22).

The question of identity is seen in the breaking of the social laws of love and bowing to the instinctual laws in the case of both mother and the daughter. Ammu disobeys the social laws of love obeying the instinctual law of the body by getting into a relationship with Velutha, an untouchable, who is junior to her by three years. Rahel discovers her husband in America and returns to Ayemenem, sharing her body with Estha, her own brother, 18 minutes junior to her: "The element of identity is seen in the breaking of the social norms in the case of both the mother and the daughter" (Barche 34).

The novel depicts women as subservient to the patriarchy without having a space of their own. The male control in the novel is absolute. The women hardly have any right over their own bodies. The progression of generations featuring Mammachi, her daughter Ammu and granddaughter Rahel reflects the degrees of control over their respective bodies. Mammachi's life seems to be controlled by Manu's dictum that in childhood a woman is under her father's control; in youth under her husband's and when her husband is dead, under her son's control without having independence (Doniger and Smith 115).

Pappachi's professional frustration finds an expression in the torture he perpetuates on his wife and daughter. Pappachi's cruelty mounts manifold with his retirement. His wife's success in the locality as a pickle and jam maker made him envious of his wife's vigour: "Pappachi, for his part, was having trouble coping with the ignominy of retirement. He was seventeen years older than Mammachi, and realised with a shock that he was an old man when his wife was still in her prime"(47).

Mammachi finally escapes the physical torments when her son Chacko arrives during vacation from England and sees his father beating her. Chacko, physically stronger than his father, overwhelms him and gives a stern warning, "I never want this to happen again" (48). Mammachi earns freedom from her servility. Roy writes:

"The day that Chacko prevented Pappachi from beating her, Mammachi packed her wife's luggage and committed it to Chacko's care. From then onwards he became the repository of all her womanly feelings. Her Man, her only Love" (168).

Mammachi suffers immensely at the hands of the patriarchal forces. The experience does not make her a rebel. She only barters one form of slavery for another. Her slavery towards her husband is replaced by her unquestioning subservience to her son. She picks up the voice of patriarchy in her relationship with her children. She is supportive of her son and adores and pampers him in all possible ways.

She even gives her new found economic independence to her son who takes over her pickle and jam factory. The transformation of 'Sophia's Tender Mangoes' has been a loss which Mammachi fails to comprehend. She is even supportive of Chacko's view about the family property: "what's your is mine and what's mine is also mine" (57). Her attitude towards her daughter, Ammu, could not be more contrasting.

It is no wonder that neither the family nor the society show any compassion for Ammu when she gets into a relationship with Velutha. When Ammu visits the police station to clear Velutha's name of the false charges, she is called and treated like a whore. Chacko does not allow her to stay with the family any more. At thirty one, she dies lonely, desolate in a cheap hotel. The violation of her body does not stop with her death. Being ex-communicated, her body cannot be buried in the church-side graveyard and has to be cremated in the government crematorium.

The patriarchal society marginalises women and makes them prisoners of their own bodies. Roy's *The God of Small Things* explores how these patriarchal forces work and voice a protest where the very body that is used for the violation of the women becomes a means of their protest.

IV

This section explores Roy's portrayal of the failure of Communism in changing the lives of the people. The novel could be read as a document on Kerala and a critique of its institutions. Roy presents in the novel the political and ideological dimensions. The communists like K.N.M. Pillai are unable to understand the conflict between their political ideology and their social attitudes to caste consciousness. Roy is critical of the comrades like Chacko and K.N.M. Pillai, who are capitalists owning Paradise Pickles and a printing press respectively.

The Dalit character Velutha is humiliated by other 'touchable' workers in the factory just because of his low caste origin. Pillai represents the deep-rooted caste prejudice prevailing in Kerala. He is proud of his wife Kalyani for not allowing a Paravan to their house. Pillai is aware of the fact that the "other Touchable resented Velutha" (121) and he waits for a time to "Iron out the wrinkle" (122).

He has no sympathy for Velutha for being tortured and killed by the police. He never tries to help him. Roy obviously blames comrades whose speech is full of unacceptable Marxist jargon but the spirit is missing, because of the collapse of the communist movement in Kerala. As regards the attitude of the communists to the untouchable, and the subhuman treatment meted out to untouchable Paravans, Roy views: "As a young boy, Velutha would come with Vellya Paapan to the back entrance of the Ayemenem House to deliver the coconuts they had plucked from the trees in the compound. Pappachi could not allow Paravans into the house. Nobody would. "They were not allowed to touch anything that Touchables touched" (73).

Velutha undergoes humiliation twice because Pillai makes use of the opportunity to suppress the workers against the management of Paradise Pickles. It is therefore an inhuman combination of casteism and communism that Roy disapproves of. Roy explains about Pillai's betrayal of Velutha and his subsequent death in Police custody: "To be fair to comrade Pillai, he did not plan the course of events that followed. He merely slipped his ready fingers into History's waiting glove. It was not entirely his fault that he lived in a society where a man's death could be more profitable than his life had ever been" (281).

Velutha, in fact excels as a craftsman in the factory. He has the ability of running the factory on his own. Being an efficient carpenter among all the workers in the factory, he is adept at operating machines. He is the first one who designs sliding-folding door in Ayemenem. Mammachi, with her strong sense of logic, also often said that "if only he hadn't been a Paravan, he might have become an engineer" (75). Velutha can repair the electronic devices like radios, clocks and water pumps. He also takes care of the plumbing work and all the electrical gadgets in the house. He is always advanced in implementing the latest technology and machines. He even repaired and established the Bharat Bottle Sealing Machine brought by Chacko from Madras.

He is capable of doing everything right from maintaining the canning machines and the pineapple slicers. He could even oil the water-pump and the small diesel generator. He also built the Aluminum sheet-lined, easy-to clean cutting surfaces, and the ground level furnaces for boiling fruit. Despite all his abilities he is maltreated by the other touchable workers of the factory. Even Mammachi, the upper caste 'Madali' does not allow him to enter the house unless there is a need of Velutha to do some favour for her.

It transcends the spatial limits to be relevant to India. Her descriptions are always concerned with unusual metaphors: whether she is describing the changed face of Meenachal River or the flower anthurium specific to Kerala or evoking the local surroundings such as the wet undergrowth, the posse of touchable policemen.

Roy describes the physical and external world focusing on local flavour and the matriarchal system, Christianity, caste system and communism. The unusual combination of casteism and communism which is a salient feature of Kerala is responsible for the horrible death of Velutha, the untouchable and a card-holding member of the communist party. The economy of Kerala underwent revolutionary change due to the wealth brought in by the foreign returnees. Roy describes: "All there were, the foreign returnees in wash 'n' wear suits and rainbow sunglasses. With an end to grinding poverty in their Aristocrat suitcases. With cement roofs for their thatched houses and geysers for their parents' bathrooms.With sewage systems and septic tanks. Maxis and high heels. Puff sleeves and lipsticks"(140).

The moving descriptions of Ayemenem reminds the local flavour of R.K. Narayan's Malgudi where he presents the life of common people. Hence, some critics read *The God of Small Things* as a regional novel.

The foregoing discussion of *The God of Small Things* makes it clear that the social institution of caste, reinforced by the religion—be it Hinduism or Cyrian Christianity—that treats the untouchables in a subhuman condition. The incident of Velutha's murder testifies that the mechanism of the state and the machinery of police together failed to alleviate the fate of the untouchable predicament of the Dalits.

Patriarchy, another important social institution not only marginalises the women, but also reduces them to the condition of objects. Finally, the communist rule in the state of Kerala proved that it failed to mitigate the miserable condition of the dalits. Thus, Arundhati Roy minces no words in being critical of the electoral form of communism, which failed to address caste, one of the seminal institutions that acted as an impediment to the development and modernisation of India as a nation.

Works Cited

Abraham, Abu. "Breaking the Love Laws." *The Hindustan Sunday Magazine,* Nov. 23, 1997. Print.

Ahmad, Aizaz. "Reading Arundhati Roy Politically." *Frontline.* Aug. 8, 1997. Print.

Beer, Gillian. Quoted by R.K. Dhawan in "Arundhati Roy: The Novelist Extraordinary."*Arundhati Roy: The Novelist Extraordinary.* Ed.R.K. Dhawan. New Delhi: Prestige, 1999. Print.

Barche, G.D. "Arundhati Roy's *The God of Small Things: Juxtaposition and Parallelism.*" *Littcrit* 25.1 and 2 (June-Dec 1999). Print.

Chekov, Anton. "To His Brother In Life and Letters." ed. and trans. S.S. Kotelionsky and Philip Tombinson. USA: Arno Press, 1886. Print.

Cowley, Jason. "Why we Chose Arundhati." *India Today* 27 Oct.1997. Print.

Cowasjee, Saros. *A Study of the Major Fiction of Mulk Raj Anand.* Delhi: OUP, 1997. Print.

Chakravarthi, Gayatri Spivak. "Can the Subaltern Speak?" *Marxism and the interpretative on of Culture.* Eds.C. Nelson and L. Grossberg. Bassingstoke: McMillan Education, 1988. Print.

Dhawan, R.K. "Arundhati Roy: The Novelist Extraordinary." *Arundhati Roy* the Novelist Extraordinary. Ed. R.K. Dawan. New Delhi: Prestige, 1999. Print.

Duits, Lind and Van Romondt Oauline. "Girls Make Sense: Girls, Celebrities and Identities." *European Journal of Cultural Studies*. Vol. 12. (2009). Print.

Doniger, Wendy and Brian K. Smith. Trans. *The Laws of Manu.* New Delhi: Penguin India, 1992. Print.

De Beauvoir, Simone. *The Second Sex.* London: Vintage classics, 1997. Print.

Gupta, G.S. Balarama. "Mulk Raj Anand's *Untouchable*: *The Dialectics of Self Affirmation."* Ed. M.K. Naik. *Perspectives on Indian Fiction on English* Delhi: Abhinav Publications, 1985. Print.

Jha, Pashupathi. *Indian Novelists in English.* Delhi: Sarup and Sons, 2000.Print.

Mc Donald, D. Edward. (Eds). *Phonex*: The Posthumous paper of D. H. Larence. New York: Viking, 1936. Print.

Mistry, Rohinton. *A Fine Balance.* London: Faber and Faber, 2003. Print.

Reddy, Ganapathi. *The Hindu.* April 19, 2002, Print.

—. *The Hindu.* April 19, 2002, Print.

Roy, Arundhati. *The God of Small Things.* New Delhi: Penguin, 1997. (All the parenthesis quotations are taken from the text).

Sharma, R.S. and Shashibala Talwar. Arundhati Roy's *The God of Small Things:* Critique and Commentary. New Delhi: Creative Books, 1998. Print.

—. Arundhati Roy's *The God of Small Things:* Critique and Commentary. New Delhi: Creative Books, 1998. Print.

Speath, A. "No Small Things" *Time,* April 14, 1997. Print.

Trivedi, Darshan. "Small is Beautiful" *In Bhatt*, 1999. Web. 20 May 2011.

Wilber, Alex. "Interview: Arundhati Roy: For me language is a skin on my thought." *The Week,* 10 Jan. 1998. Print.

Chapter - 6

'Distant Others': Immigrant Experience in *The Inheritance of Loss*

Kiran Desai's *The Inheritance of Loss* (2006), the third Booker Prize winner among the Indian English novels, is yet another work that portrays the cultural aspect of the urban India. This chapter seeks to map the multicultural aspect vis-à-vis the immigrants, a predominant theme of the recent Indian English novel. Written in four sections, the first section recounts the reception and the thematic concerns of the novel; the second section explores the multicultural concerns in the novel; the third section examines the immigrant experience as depicted in the novel; and the fourth section presents the argument of the chapter by means of conclusion.

I

Kiran Desai's *The Inheritance of Loss* was conferred the Man Booker Prize for the year 2006. The shortlist for the year include such novels as *In the Country of Men* by Hisham Matar, *The Secret River* by Kate Grenville, *Carry Me Dow* by M. J. Hyland, *Mother's Milk* by Edward St Aubyn and *The Night Watch* by Sarah Waters.

The chairman of the Booker Prize panel Hermione Lee sums up the reasons for choosing it for the award: "This is a magnificent novel of humane breadth and wisdom, comic tenderness and powerful political acuteness." (Lee web) He further added that "felt strongly about" and "admired" all the entries, and that *The Inheritance of Loss* was not a "compromise choice" (Lee). Desai's narrative provides the freshness and newness to the readers:

> A distinctive, original voice, an audacious imagination that takes readers to undiscovered countries of the mind, a strong power of storytelling and a historical truthfulness and it is a magnificent novel of human breadth and wisdom, comic tenderness and powerful political acuteness. (Mahadev web).

In her reception speech, Desai expresses a sense of overwhelm: "I didn't expect to win. I don't have a speech. My mother told me I must wear a sari...a family heirloom, but it's completely transparent! I'm Indian and so I'm going to thank my parents" (Desai Web). Commenting on Desai's *The Inheritance of Loss*, John Sutherland, Chairman of man Booker Judges 2008 aptly points out: "Desai's novel registers the multicultural reverberations of the new millennium with the sensitive instrumentality of fiction" (Sutherland xv). The multicultural reverberations are produced by the dual operations of colonisation and globalisation.

The citation of the jury and the commendation by a member of another jury of the Booker Prize seem to concur that the main concern of the novel is multiculturalism vis-à-vis immigrant experience. An attempt is made in this chapter to examine *The Inheritance of Loss* from this perspective.

The novel explores the aspects like globalisation and life in rural India. Set in New York and the Himalayas, the novel deals with an embittered judge and his desire to enjoy a peaceful retired life. Desai explains the purpose of the novel:

> I was very conscious of the emotional territory that I wanted to capture, in terms of the story, I didn't know at all what it was going to be, I think I wrote in every direction - the story of immigrants in New York, my parents, my grandparents, my journey. But yes, I was aware of the certain sort of emotional landscape, darkness, worry and fear that this journey between East and West causes. (Desai wikinews)

The novel explores childhood experiences of the writer. In the essay "The Anxiety of Indianness," Meenakshi Mukherjee offers interesting discussion on the Indian diasporic writers in English. Mukherjee contrasts "the first generation writers from the third generation writers who have greater difference in their portrayal of India focusing Indian history" (Mukherjee 86). Desai, in her portrayal of India belongs to the third generation writers.

Continuing the trend set by the third generation writers, Desai portrays India with a focus on the contemporary history beginning with her debut novel *Hullabaloo in the Guava Orchard* (1998). Though this novel received literary awards, it failed to be popular in the genre of diasporic writing in English. But her second novel *The Inheritance of Loss* has been received in the West enthusiastically for its strength of depiction and narration of the Indian history. Desai uses Raja Rao's style in terms of the portrayal of the nation. Raja Rao's famous "Foreword" to *Kanthapura* is characteristic of the self reflexivity: "The telling has not been easy. One has to convey in a language that is not one's own the spirit that is one's own. One has to convey the various shades and omissions of a certain thought movement that looks maltreated in an alien language. I use the word 'alien,' yet English is not really an alien language to us" (Rao vi).

The style that Raja Rao advocated and practiced in his works has been of immense use to the new generation writers like Salman Rushdie, Vikram Seth, Jumpa Lahiri, Kiran Desai, among others who used language for expressing the Indian sensibility. Desai applies the diasporic style to portray the Indian sensibility quite differently. The novel owes its success to the style that Desai adopted.

The Inheritance of Loss explores a large number of intriguing perspectives like post-colonialism, displacement, immigration, fundamentalism, terrorism, nationalism and globalisation. The novel explores how historical events can have adverse influence on the lives of the people. The impact in turn has bearing on the subsequent generations. Desai is interested in the post-1980s India.

The novelist employs the omniscient narrative. By doing so, she helps the readers understand multiple perspectives. The subject matter of the novel attracted the attention of the Western readers. Desai captures the shifts in time with great ease. Events of the past such as the Judge's early life and marriage, or details of Sai's parents and her childhood are treated as flashbacks of the characters. The atmosphere of Kalimpong and of Biju's life in New York is built up through minor characters. Both the strands of the narrative are made to have a psychological realism.

The density of the aspects of the novel is indicated through the title: the word 'loss' relates to what the people miss in the contemporary life. In the epigraph, Desai sates: 'My humanity is in feeling we are all voices of the same poverty…my name is someone and anyone. I walk slowly, like one who comes from far away he does not expect to arrive" (Jorge 1). The epigraph stresses the idea that man's only inheritance in this life is one of poverty of various kinds, material and spiritual. Ultimately one can only strive for, but never actually attain, fulfillment.

Desai explores the aspects of 'inheritance' and 'loss.' The loss of Sai's father, an Air Force officer, who is about to become the first Indian to fly into space is moving. His loss is due to his untimely demise in an accident along with his wife in Moscow. Sai, aged six is admitted to the convent school which she apparently hates. Sai becomes an orphan. Her father, who was brought up in a Zoroastrian charity for orphans, was an orphan.

Sai's mother was disowned by her parents, because she runs away with a Parsi boy and gets married against the will of her parents. Thus, the tradition of orphanage continued through three generations in the family. This leads to a sense of rootlessness, which is inherited from generation to generation.

Sai inherits the rootlessness of her parents after their death. She is sent to live with her maternal grandfather, who is a judge. Sai's first night at the grandfather's house in Kalimpong is an insulting and intimidating experience. The novel begins with the idyllic description of north-eastern Himalayan scene: "All day, the colours had been those of dusk, mist moving like a water creature across the great flanks of mountains possessed of ocean shadows and depths. Briefly visible above the vapour, Kanchenjunga was a far peak whittled out of rice, gathering the last of the light" (1).

Set in mid-1980's at Kalimpong, the novel portrays life at the foot of mount Kanchenjunga in the North-Eastern part of post-independence India. A retired judge, Jemubhai Patel lives with his cook and his orphaned granddaughter Sai and his pet dog, Mutt. Although the novel is set in two different places completely, the action is engineered by the presence of the Judge and cook's Son Biju in New York. He keeps changing the restaurants as a cook. He changes his work places in order to get permanent permission as a resident in the USA.

Numerous incidents take place in Kalimpong due to regional disputes between the Indo-Nepali insurgency. In the beginning, the young Indian-Nepali insurgents enter the house of Jemubhai. They steal the Judge's guns and forces him to offer snacks by humiliating him. The judge is made to say "Jai Ghorkha," "Jai Jai Ghorkha." The Indo-Nepalis are tired of being treated as minority in their own area where they are in large number. They want at least their own state if not their own country.

As the police arrive, the cook lives in a small hut in the village. The police find a series of letters written by the cook to his son Biju in the USA. The letters intrigue the police conveying the story of immigrants who face ordeals due to lack of opportunities in America. The reading of the letters gives two contrastive cultures—Indian and American, an aspect explored in detail in the following section.

II

This section examines the multicultural concerns of the novel. The story moves back and forth contrasting two cultures. The first strand of the story moves from India to America with a description of the cook's son who stays in America. The second strand moves from England to India dealing with the male protagonist, Jemubhai Patel. The description of Jemubhai's success overwhelms his community because he is the first person from their community to do so. His father, Bamanbhai, a rich man of the Patel community, finds a good looking girl to his son. Married to the Indian girl, Jemubai turns out to be unhappy because of the negative impact of the multiculturalism.

Jemubhai, when he starts working in India, loves the authority and power of his position as a touring official. He would go and measure the fields in style. Though a retired official, his position still gives him authority and power as can be gauged from the remark of the police officer who opines that the robbery of guns from a retired member of the Indian Civil Services cannot be ignored. But as the agitation for Gorkhaland continues and becomes serious, leading even to bloodshed, the established hierarchy is discarded.

The people in the post-colonial India need to strive and get their due. They often become aggressive. For example, Lola complains to the head of the Kalimpong wing of the Gorkha National Liberation Front (GNLF) called Pradhan. When he learns that he has a French name, he retorts: "I didn't know we live in France. Do we? Tell me, why don't I speak in French, then?" (243). He did not look at the papers of her property which gave the measurements of the plot. He told her that his men had to be accommodated. When Lola tried to continue the conversation he becomes insolent: "I am the raja of Kalimpong. A raja must have many queens" he jerked his head back to the sounds of the kitchen that came through the curtained door. "I have four, but would you," he looked Lola up and down" (244).

The misogyny of Jemubhai Patel needs to be understood as an instance of multicultural influence on him. He feels that he is forced to stay on the interface of English and Indian cultures. Educated at Bishop Cotton School, he developed a profound veneration for the portrait of Queen Victoria that stands at the school's entrance. Jemubhai's reverences for the colonial masters could be considered one of the reasons for marrying a woman who brings him dowry.

He ignores the conjugal life with his wife at home. Jemubhai's attempt to internalise the culture of the colonisers is noted in a transcendental choice-freeze. Though he inherited glorious Indian culture, he does not use it as a frame of reference. Jemubhai instead attempts to internalise the culture of the colonisers.

The imitation of the West results in the inauthentic self of Jemubhai. He realises that in the process of learning a foreign way of life, he has become the mimic man. However, he would not acknowledge it: "He wouldn't tumble his pride to melodrama to the end of his life and he knew the danger of confession- it would cancel any hope of dignity forever" (208).

Therefore, he decides to buy Cho Oyu, a house built by a Scotsman in the north-eastern Himalayas. He feels that the location of the house gives him a shelter. The house is a means of escape for him. He is culturally alienated from the native people. He can hardly speak the tongue of the common people of Kalimpong. Therefore, he does not develop any psychic and cultural relation with the people. He hates his wife to the extent that he developed misanthropy: "He did not like his wife's face, searched for his hatred, found beauty, and dismissed it, once it had been a terrifying beckoning thing that had made his heart turn water. An Indian girl never be as beautiful as an English one..." (168-69).

Nimi however begins to protest against the inhuman behaviour of Jemubhai. The hatred needs to be understood as a result of the cultural differences. He never speaks and looks for direction. She was uncared for. Her freedom is useless and her husband disregarded his duty. He calls her lazy, wide as a buffalo. These physical and mental tortures make her invalid. She begins falling asleep during day and wakes up in the middle of the night. Jemubhai's tortures create dislike to see her in the mirror because she could not see herself in it. Because of the psychological tortures of Jemubhai, her cheeks erupt.

He considers her a fallen beauty as a further affront. He is scared of touching her due to her skin disease. To top it all, he discourages and orders her not to show herself outside lest people might run away from her seeming. This is how the novelist makes Jemubhai a misogynist and a degrading selfish animal. She stays in her sister's house in which she burns herself to death while cooking.

The novelist sums up the brutal picture of Jemubhai: "Now Jemubhai wondered if he had killed his wife for the sake of false ideals. Stolen her dignity, shamed his family, shamed hers, turned her into the embodiment of their humiliation" (308). As for his daughter: "he had condemned the girl to convent boarding schools. She relieved herself when she reached a new height of uselessness and absurdity by eloping with a man who had grown up in an orphanage" (308).

Multiculturalism in the context of globalisation has such bearing on the urban populace that the inherent conflict between the native culture and the Western culture is difficult to be resolved, and the genre of the Indian English novel represents this aspect effectively. *The Inheritance of Loss* in this respect is a landmark publication in representing the aspect of multiculturalism.

III

This section examines the immigrant experience as portrayed in *The Inheritance of loss.* An attempt to understand the theory of inter-cultural influences would help understand the novel better. Globalisation celebrates inter-cultural influences, which Frederic Jameson terms "postmodern celebration of difference and differentiation" (Jameson 77).

This incident takes place when almost all the cultures of the world come into contact with one another. The contact, however, is not always direct. Often it acts as a distance, "whereby the actions of social agents in one locale can come to have significant consequences for distant others" (Held and Grew 50).

The 'distant others' are, of course the people of the Third World, who come under the influence of the culture of the first world. The immigrants feel the direct influences of globalisation. The immigrants, in their attempt to come to terms with a foreign culture in a foreign land, become fractured images of life. Salman Rushdie explains: "Human beings (immigrants) do not perceive things whole; we are not gods but wounded creatures, cracked lenses, capable only of fractured perceptions" (Rushdie 56).

Desai thus is preoccupied with the themes of dislocation, invasion, empire building and migration. She defeats the sense of loss of the dispossessed and the pangs felt by separation. Tessa Hadley remarks: "Cho Oyu is a tragic-comic metaphor for the seedy remains of British imperial culture in India. It is suggestive too of the novel form itself, another alien habit that might at first glance seem as ill-matched to its Indian environment as the stodgy meals and ideas about keeping up civilisation" (Hadley 25-26).

The novelist portrays different phases of Indian migration to the European countries. The first wave of migrants reached there for higher studies. Jemubhai Patel represents this stream. He leaves for Cambridge to pursue higher education. Mala Pandurang writes in this regard: "Yet despite his unhappiness as an alien in England, he envies the English and loathes Indians and grows increasingly embittered by the translation realisation that he would be despised by absolutely everyone, English and India both" (Pandurang 94).

In *Postcolonial Transformation*, Bill Ashcroft argues that "place is always more than mere location for the subject whose identity is in crisis...The sense of 'place-ness' is vulnerable to violent intervention, however, because it entails dwell(ing) in a space beyond (mere) location, an imaginative space deeply imbued with the place-ness of (one's) own carefully nurtured sense of being" (Ashcroft 158).

Commenting on the place-ness, Michael de Certeau views that 'place-ness' will denote not just the physical locale of home and home-region, but also a person's emotional, legal, aesthetic and existential investment in a given physical location. "Places are fragmentary and inward-turning...that others are not allowed to read" (Certeau 68). Place-ness can therefore be understood as the historical presence, both personal and social. It often entails a sense of ownership, sometimes in the sense of private property, sometimes in the sense of belonging to a place. It does not, however entail an abstract knowledge.

The sense of place-ness in the novel results from disturbances and dislocation. The main events of the novel take place in a mountainous region of India with a temperate climate and loose topsoil.

These conditions lead to frequent landslides, especially in the monsoon season. The imminent threat of the landslides clearly destabilises the permanence of human structures. A few instances of the landslides in the text show how the phenomenon destabilises place, rendering Kalimpong and nearby regions more like empty space.

The older members of the group declare that Darjeeling is barely recognisable, that it has "gone downhill in more ways than one. It has become a place of confusion and noise" (197). The landslides are linked to societal decay and poor land management. There is a shortage of room for the exploding population, but instead of more permanent solutions, the local government advises building rickety additions to the buildings. The reader is not privy to the after effects of the Darjeeling landslides forecasted by the narrator.

Later, when Sai's neighbour Lola visits Pradhan, the head of the GNLF in Kalimpong, she attempts to use the very real threat of landslides to clear her home of Gorkha squatters. She remarks to Pradhan that his followers have "cut into the hill, land weak, landslide may occur…very dangerous for your men Landslide on road" (244). The threat of landslides is laid to excess and selfishness. Lola exaggerates the danger in order to scare the GNLF people off her property, but her threat can only be made in the context of perennial landslides in the Kalimpong region.

The violence in the novel functions as a means to break down place-ness into liminal space with the aim of rebuilding place to the aggressor's specifications. There is always some kind of scope for people who live in the peaceful provinces. Different parties can have different feelings of place within a given location. The competitive nature of place-ness is therefore evident in the historical record, as well as in Desai's novel. Lola employs pedagogic approach to understanding Kalimpong history and her privileged place in its current society: "All of [a] sudden, all that they had claimed innocent, fun, funny, not really to matter, was proven wrong. It *did* matter…They had pretended it didn't, or had nothing to do with them, and suddenly it had everything to do with them" (242).

Lola and Noni, the sisters understand that they "had been wrong. The real place had evaded them. The two of them had been fools; they were doing something exciting just by occupying this picturesque cottage" (247). The sisters' sense of place-ness has been destabilised. The narrator's use of the verb 'occupying' offers clear motif of the unlawful tenancy. A noted critic, Ganguly in this regard writes: "GNLF drags the privileged Kalimpong inhabitants, among whom Desai once counted her own family into the liminal space between the pedagogical and the performative, not letting the wealthy plead innocent for inevitably inheriting a greater portion of wealth" (Ganguly 472).

The idea of nationhood is often based on pride in native culture. Indian identity is multiple and is complicated further by the colonial influences. Sai Mistry, the main female character in the novel says: "What was a country but the idea of it? She thought of India as concept, a hope or a desire. How often could you attack before it is crumbled?" (236). The characters are stunted by their whimsical situations with the West. The judge has been to England as a student but gets isolated.

The coloured colonisers compel in their desperate bid to imitate the white colonisers. Thus they become impoverished specimens of people who are almost the same as the colonial masters, but not the same. Homi Bhabha would describe this kind of colonialism: "almost the same but not white" (Bhabha 35).

The mimic women, living within the interfaces of two cultures, develop split identities. They hate to imitate, but cannot help imitating. This ruined mimetic effort obviously causes in the creation of frustrated men and women who cannot come to terms with themselves as well as with the society.

The characters in the novel are exposed to different cultures in Kalimpong. The Anglicized Sai learns at an early age that "Cake is better than laddoos" (33). Sai interacts with the cook in a code mixed languages of English and Hindi. Culturally she does not match with Gyan who is more interested in celebrating Guru Nanak's birthday, Durga Puja or the Tibetan New Year than Christmas that interests Sai. Desai depicts the cultural collision between Gyan and Sai. Frustrated, Gyan reacts: "You are like slaves, that's what you are, running after the west embarrassing yourself" (163).

Desai seems to set up an inverse co-relation between the material success that the characters strike and their ethical aspects. Materially, one of the most successful characters in the novel is that of the judge. Biju ends up materially as one of the poorest characters in the novel. But his love for his father reflects that his heart is in the right place. Desai anglicizes the names of the characters like Harish-Harry, Gaurish-Gary and Dhansuk-Danny to reveal the co-existence of the occidental and oriental cultures.

Harish, the owner of a café, hates his white customers. He wants to break their necks. His daughter, however is Americanised. Tejinder Kaur writes in this regard: "Commonalities of experience of...the legal and illegal Diaspora communities and individuals in America as well as by the people from other states, regions and communities from India residing in Kalimpong" (Kaur 98).

Desai depicts the mindset of the anglicised class of the Indian society. The portions of the novel that deal with the life of Lola and Noni reveal this aspect. Desai drifts into the minute particularities of their life, and gets all the details just right, including the names: "And finally there was Noni, who lived with her sister Lola in a rose-covered cottage named Mon Ami. When Lola's husband had died of a heart attack, Noni, the spinster, had moved in with her sister, the widow. They lived on his pension being done to the house" (41-42). Immigrant experience thus plays havoc with the lives of those who are indiscriminate in allowing themselves susceptible.

IV

It has been argued in the foregoing sections that Desai portrays in the novel the cultural aspect of the urban India with a focus on the multicultural aspect vis-à-vis the immigrant experience. Her portrayal of the characters explores the multicultural concern and immigrant experience.

The style that Raja Rao advocated and practiced in his works has been of immense use to the new generation writers like Salman Rushdie, Vikram Seth, Jumpa Lahiri, Kiran Desai, among others who used language for expressing the Indian sensibility. Desai applies the diasporic style to portray the Indian sensibility quite differently. *The Inheritance of Loss* owes its success to the style that Desai adopted.

To suit her theme and concerns, Desai adeptly employs the experiments in the case of the language. Her creative use of English contributed to the effectiveness of the novel. Sounds are reproduced to create necessary effect. Expressions such as 'the rustling of the wind and grass,' 'the twittering of birds,' 'the croaking of the frogs,' 'the whistling of the owl,' 'the ringing of the phone,' 'the bowling of taxi horns,' among others are effective because of the sound. Besides, Desai employs exclamations from Hindi and other vernaculars: 'Arre, chala, chalo, 'Bilkul bekaar,' 'bepkhup.' Oddities in pronunciation are captured through deliberate mis-spelling as in 'naaty boy,' 'daallars,' 'ahffend,' 'Ah'm,' 'whaat,' 'whaat,' 'deeference,' 'telephone,' 'haeve..'

Even the sing song voice or drawling tone of the speaker is captured admirably as in "'maroooooooned' (100), 'bee-oo-tee-ful' country (131), care for a drop of sh-e-rr-y, mye dee-a-r? (152). Elsewhere too with astounding success the novelist can teach the very inflection of voice as in 'poetatio,' 'Toematto' *(*131). Highly entertaining instances of ungrammatical English are sampled through expressions, phrases and jumbled up sentences such as the following: 'No speak English,' (267) 'But he work here. His mother tell us,' (96) 'I ask you nicely, Go,' (96) 'Where she live with three *Friends*, everyone go shopping *separately, separately* they cook their dinner, *together* they eat their *separate* food… she put her name on the box so it say who it belong to! In Zanzibar what one person have *he have to share with everyone*...But then everyone have nothing, man! That is why I leave Zanzibar" (98).

The speech of the English-educated upper class Indian women in America too figures in the story through "*Namaste,* Kusum Auntie. *Aayiye, baethiye, khayiye"!* (50) Other devices adopted by the novelist to lend authenticity are the use of block letters to indicate high pitched voice and a deliberate omission of punctuation marks to convey a sense of breathless narration evident in the typical reeling off of the menu by a waiter in a restaurant: 'Mutton curry,' 'mutton pulao,' 'vegetable curry' and 'vegetable pulao.'

The expressions such as 'postage stamp mirror,' (147) 'refrigerated voice,' (257) and 'cockroachery desire' (299) strike the reader with their originality. The descriptions like the following are noteworthy for their felicity and poetic imaginativeness: 'the world resembled a map from a divine perspective' (141); 'moving an expressionless face like a sunflower' (143); 'Jemubhai's new second-hand car. Looked more like a friendly stout cow than an automobile' (172); 'Rent a room in someone else's life' (213); 'lived soft birds flying you could let the words free' (200).

The foregoing discussion of Desai's *The Inheritance of Loss* with a focus on the portrayal of the cultural aspect of the urban India is suggestive that the novel represents an important aspect of modern India. An attempt has been made to map the multicultural aspect vis-à-vis the immigrants. In this respect, *The Inheritance of Loss* occupies an important place in the genre of the recent Indian English novel.

Works Cited

Ashcroft, Bill. *Post-colonial Transformation.* London: Routledge, 2001. Print.

—. *Post-colonial Transformation.* London: Routledge, 2001. Print.

—. Gareth Griffiths and Helen Tiffin. *Key Concepts in Post Colonial Studies.* London: Routledge, 1998. Print.

Borge, Luis Jorge. "Boast Of Quiteness." *Literary Jewels.* 17. Jan. 2008. Web. 16 Dec. 2011.

Bhabha, Homi. *Nation and Narration.* London: Routledge, 1994. Print.

—. *Nation and Narration.* London: Routledge, 1994. Print.

—. *Nation and Narration.* London: Routledge, 1994. Print.

"Foreword to Kanthapura." Introduction. *Kanthapura* by Raja Rao. Bombay: OUP, 1947. Print.

Ganguly. "Poverty Malgovernance and Ethnopolitical Mobilisation." Web. 12. Oct. 2011.

Jameson, Frederic. "Notes on Globalisation as a philosophic Issue." *The Cultures of Globalisation."* Eds. Frederic Jameson and Masso Miyoshi. Durham: Duke University Press, 1998. Print.

Kaur, Tejinder. "Problematizing Issues about Home, Homeland, Diaspora and belongingness in Transnational and national land: A Study of Kiran Desai's *The Inheritance of Loss."* Quoted in Reena Mitra. "Anatomising Immigrant Lives: Kiran Desai's *The Inheritance of Loss.*" Critical Responses to Kiran Desai. Eds. Sunita Sinha and Bryan Reynolds. New Delhi:Atlantic Publishers and Distributors, 2009.Print.

"Kiran Desai wins Man Booker"—*CNN-IBN*, October 11, 2006. Web. 12. Dec. 2011.

Lee, Hermione. Wikinews online. Web. 20 Dec. 2011.

Meenakshi, Mukharjee.*The Perishable Empire: Essays on Indian Writing in English.* OUP, 2000. Print.

—. *The Perishable Empire: Essays on Indian Writing in English.* OUP, 2000. Print.

Panduranga, Mala. "Loss and Longing" Rev of *The Inheritance of Loss.*" *The Book Review* 30 - 5 (May 2006). Print.

Rushdie, Salman. *Imaginary Homelands.* London: Granta Books, 1991. Print.

Tessa, Hadley. "Exotic to Whom?" Rev of *The Inheritance of Loss. London Review Books* 28 - 19 (Oct. 2006). Print.

"Wiki/Kiran. Web. 20. Dec. 2011.

http://www.alibris.com/blog/alibris/kiran-desai-wins-man-booker- prize-for-fiction 26.Dec. 2011.

http://articles.timesofindia.indiatimes.com/2006-10- 11/world/27819506_1_ kiran-desai-man-booker-prize-short- listed . 26.Dec. 2011

http://articles.timesofindia.indiatimes.com/2006-10-11/world/27819506_1_ kiran-desai-man-booker-prize-short- listed.27.Dec. 2011

Chapter - 7

Representation of Modern India: Social Contexts in *The White Tiger*

This chapter attempts to explore Aravind Adiga's *The White Tiger* (2008) with a focus on the social aspect of modern India. The model of interpretation adopted in the chapter has been Lisa Lau's concept of 're-Orientalism,' according to which the critique of modern India is developed not by the Western intelligentsia as in the case of Orientalism but the liberal Indian intelligentsia. *The White Tiger* is interpreted in the chapter as an attempt of 're-Orientalism' on the part of its author.

Written in four sections, the first section of the chapter explores the reception of the novel and the thematic concerns of the novel; the second section deals with the representation of modern India with special reference to the chief protagonist in the social contexts of feudal oppression, casteism and dalit suppression; the third section focuses on the individual's growth and its use of the *Bildungsroman* and subjectivity; the fourth section sums up the argument stating that the novel is about individualism rather than collectivism; of personal growth rather than the growth in the community.

I

Adiga won the prestigious Man Booker Prize for his very first novel *The White Tiger*. The other novels shortlisted for the coveted Prize include: Amitav Ghosh's *Sea of Poppies*, Sebastian Barry's

The Secret Scriptures, Linda Grant's *The Clothes on Their Backs*, Philip Hensher's *The Northern Clemency* and Steve Toltz's *A Fraction of the Whole.*

The novel has been appreciated for its density of experience and innovative narrative technique: "In many ways it was the perfect novel," comments Michael Portillo, chairman of the judges' panel, "the novel undertakes an extraordinary task—he gains and holds the attention of the reader for a hero who is a thoroughgoing villain." The main criterion for the prize, he said, was: "Does this book knock my socks off? And this did" (Charlotte 3).

The judges found it a difficult decision to select the novel for the prize: "It was pretty close to other novels," Portillo continues, "in the end, *The White Tiger* overtook the others because the judges felt that it shocked and entertained in equal measure." Portillo draws a parallel with *Macbeth*: "It is about ambition realised through murder," he said, "but with a delicious twist. Whereas Lady Macbeth and Macbeth are driven mad by their crime, the hero of this book is only driven mad by the fact that he hesitated and might not have committed his crime" (Charlotte 3-4).

The novel received overwhelming response from the readers, critics and scholars. Critics have been generous in showering praise on the book and its author. Claimed as extraordinary and brilliant, thrilling and insightful, witty and unpretentious, the novel is considered one of the most powerful books published in the genre of recent Indian English novel:

> As a debut, it marks the arrival of a storyteller who strikes a fine balance between the sociology of the wretched place he has chosen as theme and the twisted humanism of the outcast...The ruthlessness of power and survival assumes a million moral ambiguities in this novel. (Prasannarajan 63).

What is unique about the novel is that the author portrays the double standards of the nation in respect of the rich and the poor. For this purpose, the author employs the technique of black humour. Black humour projects the story in an invincible sense of disillusionment and cynicism, with little or no hope of escape to the protagonists.

Jacqueline and Mary Beth explain in this connection: "When black comedy is used as a basis for a story's plotline, it involves a society in an unhealthy state...The audience should usually be able to see this for themselves, and often a supporting character within the story also sees the insanity of the situation. (Jacqueline and Beth 175-76).

Adiga uses this genre to challenge the fascinating journey of the nation towards development. The novelist critiques the startling reality of a nation where unplanned and haphazard urbanisation and colonisation causes suffocation leading to poverty, corruption, disease and moral degeneration.

The plot of the novel being simple, moves back and forth. Adiga's novel explores the darker side of India's rise to prosperity through its narrator, the son of a rickshaw puller, who escapes crushing poverty. It centres round Balram Halwai, who experiences the ordeals of life due to casteism and feudalism. The novel makes use of the epistolary style.

Adiga's concern for the main character, who belongs to the low caste in the village called Laxmangarh is commendable. Laxmangarh, birthplace of the main character, is introduced to the leaders as a "typical Indian village paradise" with its school as a paradise within a paradise. Balram considers himself as born and raised in darkness. Darkness is used as description for a place that is away from Bodh Gaya.

Adiga describes how the modern India exists in ten thousand years as a rooster coop: "Hundreds of pale hens and brightly coloured roosters, stuffed tightly into wire mesh cages, packed as tightly as worms in a belly, pecking each other and shitting on each other, jostling just for breathing shape: the whole cage giving off a horrible stench the stench of terrified flesh" (173).The rooster coop in the novel is symbolic of the poor. It also stands for the human beings, who are looked down upon merely as animals without having a heart and a soul. The novel attempts to show the ingrained prejudice meted out to the poor on the basis of caste discrimination:

> Go to Old Delhi, behind the Jama Masjid, and look at the way they keep chickens there in the market. Hundreds of pale hens and

> brightly coloured roosters, stuffed tightly into wire-mesh cages, packed as tightly as worms in a belly, pecking each other and shitting on each other, jostling just for breathing space; the whole cage giving off a horrible stench the stench of terrified, feathered flesh. (173-74).

Towards the end of the novel, Balram proclaims that he has broken free of this rooster coop situation. The reader knows that it is not on account of a moral vision or growth but due to the twist of the writer's cynical tone. The novel abounds in instances of pessimistic, gloomy and derisory humour. There appears to be no meaning in their existence except that they live in The Great Indian Rooster Coop.

II

This section examines the representation of India with special reference to the chief protagonist in the social contexts of feudal oppression, casteism and dalit suppression. It is argued in the section that the poor are like the pale hens trapped in the coop. They fail to protest. They grow up without self awareness and self realisation of what they need. The poor man's tragic life lies in the fact that he has to continue living in pathetic conditions.

The nation happens to be an important aspect of representation in the Indian English novel. Meenakshi Mukherjee writes about the chief concerns of the novelists: "The nation is a central metaphor in the tradition of the Indian novel in English since the history of the Independence of India from British power and the formation of the nation constitute an ideological and emotional process that deeply affected the whole subcontinent" (Mukherjee 43).

The first generation novels have been supported because they resist the orientalists' representation of Indian cultural identity as inferior to the West. The novelists of the second generation created great controversy because they problematise the Indian religious and social identities. There is a long line of Indian novels in English addressing these second issues such as Mulk Raj Anand's *Untouchables* (1935), Arundhati Roy's *The God of Small Things* (1997) and Adiga's *The White Tiger*.

The aspect of social identity is represented through the parable of the servant-master relationship in *The White Tiger*. Speaking on the servant master relationship, Adiga writes:

> The servant-master system implies two things: one is that the servants are far poorer than the rich. A servant has no possibility of ever catching you to the master. And secondly, has access to the master- the master's money, the master's physical person. Yet crime rates in India are very low. Even though the middle class...are paranoid about crime, the reality is a master getting killed by his servant. (231).

Balram is presented as a modern Indian hero in the midst of the economic prosperity of India in the recent past. He climbs up the ladder of success by murdering Mr Ashok, his employer. He steals his bagful of money. His decision to kill is based on the philosophy of revenge, ambition and corruption.

Balram is the representative of the poor in India. His story is a parable of the new India with a distinctly macabre twist. Kapur Akash comments: "He is not only an entrepreneur but also a roguish criminal remarkably capable of self-justification. The background against which he operates is one of corruption, inequality and poverty" (Akash 7). Adiga highlights the ever widening gap between the rich and the poor and the economic system that lets a small minority to prosper at the expense of the majority. Raaj opines: "At time when India is going through great changes and, with China, likely to inherit the world from the West, it is important that writers like me try to highlight the brutal injustices of society...the great divide" (Raaj 9).

Ever since the neo-liberal economic reforms were introduced in India, there has been greater economic disparity. There is a growing consumption by the rich and the urban upper middle income groups. Side by side, the lives of the poor become vulnerable and precarious. Jean Dreze and Amartya Sen examine the achievements and limitations of the Indian democracy. They comment on the adverse effects of the social inequality. They point out how the quality of democracy is often compromised by social inequality and inadequate political participation, though democratic practice itself is a powerful tool of elimination of social inequality (Dreze 37). *The White Tiger* may be understood as a fictionalised version of what Drez and Amrtya Sen describe.

The title of *The White Tiger* is symbolically used in order to represent the new India. The novelist offers the meaning of the white tiger: "....the rarest of animals-the creature that comes along only once in a generation?" (35). The meaning of the novel itself gives a clear cut idea that it is an exhaustive struggle for low caste people to break out of their oppressive cultural background of upper caste domination and to seek success from this. It also suggests that only a small percentage of poor people prosper in their lives. Adiga also portrays the socio-economic and political conditions of the post-globalised India.

The novelist attempts to show the inefficiency of the Indian administration and political leaders who dominate in all aspects to show their power and the common man's problems after its independence. Meenakshi Mukherjee writes: "The nation is a central metaphor in the tradition of the Indian novel in English since the history of the independence of India from British power and the formation of the nation constitute an ideological and emotional process that deeply affected the whole subcontinent" (Mukherjee 43-44).

Adiga's juxtaposition of the main character's personality is remarkable in the novel. The personality of the character has been changed from immaturity and innocence to successful entrepreneur. India represents the poor people whose life is conditioned: "no drinking water, no electricity, no sewage system, no public transportation, no sense of hygiene, courtesy or punctuality." (4) The functioning of school is defunct, teachers are mired in corruption, as they do not get their salaries regularly. They use allocated money to books and uniforms. The natural resources are mainly owned by the local mafia and the people have to beg for jobs. The members of big families are constantly at each other's throats. India is contrasted with the rich and the poor.

The novelist interprets the political system and bureaucratic set up in the country. The novel refers to the darkest areas of India which breed "rottenness and corruption..." (50) hampering all the developmental and welfare schemes. It restricts half of this country from achieving its potential. Most of the politicians are "half baked. That's the whole tragedy of this country" (10).

The story of Balram's emergence is the instance of the success of a common man. Government doctors, entrepreneurs, taxpayers, industrialists in India are befriended with ministers to fulfill their vested interests. Even Mukesh and Ashok also bribe the minister to settle income tax accounts. Adiga considers, "Typhoid, cholera and election fever are the three main diseases of this country and the last one the worst" (98).

According to Adiga, the voters discuss the issue of elections helplessly as "eunuchs discuss the *Kama Sutra*." (98) Apart from it, Adiga also examines the social and religious conditions in an engrossing manner as it happened in the novel due to the corrupted system in the country.

All these aspects are based on the caste lines between the haves and the have-nots. Adiga quotes: "To sum up-in the old days there were one thousand castes and destinies in India. In the modern context of India, there are two castes: men with Big Bellies, and men with Small bellies, and only two destinies: eat and eaten up" (64).

Indians are divided on caste lines: "To sum up-in the old days there were one thousand castes and destinies in India. In the modern context of India there are two castes: "Men with Big Bellies, and men with Small Bellies, and only two destinies: eat and eaten up" (64). The novelist's irony brings out the fact that the present India and in the era of globalisation, the entire system appears to be owned by the capitalist rules of the fittest of the survival.

Adiga depicts in the novel the other side of India. Amitava Kumar, however finds *The White Tiger* inauthentic and points out how several non-resident Indian authors after Rushdie had taken refuge in magic realism and have gone farther into inauthenticity. (Kumar 2).

Gayatri Chakravorty Spivak's concept of Subaltern leads to the premise that subaltern cannot speak. Subaltern signifies proletarian, whose voice could not be heard, being structurally written out of the capitalist bourgeois narrative (Kilburn 25).

Through Balram, Adiga represents the typical psychopath that the society can churn out. In "Behavioural Traits of Psychopaths," Jennifer Copley points out: "While most people's actions are guided by a number of factors, such as the desire to avoid hurting other people, the psychopath selects a course of action based on only one factor—what can he get out of it. This cold-blooded mode of reasoning enables the psychopath to commit acts that most people's consciences would not allow" (Copley 31).

Psychopaths, in the sense Copley used, are also known as 'sociopaths' who are manipulative, deceitful, impulsive lacking self-restraint and inclined to take risks. They are "Callous, deceitful, reckless, guiltless…The psychopath understands the wishes and concerns of others; he simply does not care…The psychopath believes that rules and morals are for others, weaker people who obey because they fear punishment." (Adams 12) These traits are found in Balram who goes about heroically planning his heinous crimes.

Adiga problematises casteism, dalit-suppression and marginalisation of the protagonist, who has been suppressed both psychologically and physically in all the realms of life by Ashok. Interestingly, Adiga's depiction of Balram Ashok—the oppressed and the oppressor—correspond with the roles that Ashish Nandy discusses in *The Intimate Enemy* in terms of the colonised India and the colonising British.

Balram possesses what Nandy describes as the most important quality of the downtrodden, "the passive and feminine' of the weak victimised, surviving outer pressures by refusing to overplay his sense of autonomy and self-respect" and who "in his non-heroic ordinariness…is the archetypal survivor" (Nandy 111). On the other hand, the oppressor Ashok and his wife Pinky possess what Nandy calls the "Dionysian aspect of the modern west…the demonic self for *asura Prakriti*" (Nandy 78).

The relationship between Balram and Ashok correspond to the exploited-exploiter relationship. The employee and employer relationship is markedly unequal in the novel. Balram is very weak and Ashok very strong. Thus, the employee is always subordinate to the employer. The novelist shows how Balram's education, or lack of it, is due to his low caste background. He had to quit school, in spite of being the brightest boy in his class, and has to take up work in a tea stall as a dishwasher so as to raise money and clear his family's debts.

He has been honoured by the teachers in excelling in his studies in the school. At school the school inspector offers him a scholarship that enables Balram to lessen his financial burden. Balram seeks a cultural identity. The marginalised life of the main character results in becoming a rebellion against his owner as an individual.

Balram's rebellion is not only against the members of the upper caste, but also of his own caste. Adiga criticises the caste system by projecting how the people from the upper caste victimise those of the lower caste. He depicts how an individual's own caste can become stifling. Parekh Bikhu writes that the identity-based group is central in the sense that "it shelters the individual against the humiliations of the wider society" (Bikhu 49).

Adiga does not romanticise the poor or appeal to the reader's compassion. He explores how the family sucks the blood of its men, and keeps them to the poorly paid jobs permitted by their caste. The protagonist is reluctant to accept the job assigned by his caste, that of sweet maker, that as he ironically points out, has nothing to do with the profession it indicates but means becoming another personality a starved man from the darkness, working in a tea shop for a pittance.

Apart from caste domination, the feudalism made the character very wild and rebellious and searching for his own identity. In order to break free from social suppression imposed by the owners, Balram became wild and rebellious and he violates the dichotomy of traditional life between servant and landlord to expect a new role, that of an entrepreneur.

Adiga depicts the protagonist's revenge in murdering his employer whose life is influenced by the western culture to look upon the servants very badly as he thinks everything is expected to happen within no time. Moreover, the owner, Mr Ashok tends to forget the economic and political conditions of the country being away from the motherland and addicted to foreign life.

All the comforts lead to fall into the mockery of his servants: “He was a weak, helpless, absent-minded, and completely unprotected by the usual instincts that run in the blood of a landlord” (120). The so called white tiger life is freed from the shackles when he takes up violence - murdering his beloved owner and stealing his money.

III

This section examines the growth of the individual and the use of the *Bildungsroman.* The focus of the section is on subjectivity of the protagonist Balram. An attempt to know about the subjectivity helps understand the shaping of the protagonist. Subjectivity is shaped by personal experience: “Subjectivity is determined by the processing of individuals, which is shaped by personal experience. Moreover, it can be reflected in one’s decisions to adhere to social rules. Key elements that form one’s subjectivity, then, is crucial to the presentation and development of their mode of communication” (Richard web).

Adiga employs the *Bildungsroman* as a technique to suggest the growth of the character into a mature man. The progression of the character from childhood to maturity helps understand Balram’s decisions. His poverty does not come in the way of reaching the maturity level. Balram is an omniscient, clever and unusual narrator. The narration is half-real and half-dreamy. The technique of *Bildungsroman* draws the attention of the readers to the protagonist’s arduous and agonising journey.

He suffers both physical and psychological torture. He confronts many obstacles and challenges meted out by the dominant norms of the social order. Eventually, he learns to adapt his desires and aspirations. Joseph Slaughter explains: “The journey ends with the hero as a fully socialised, normalised, and incorporated member of his society.”(Slaughter 25) While the genre is distinctively European, Adiga appropriates the model suitably.

The *Bildungsroman* concept explains Balram's progression of his career from village life to a successful entrepreneur. His sudden growth from low caste community to higher position is significant. Adiga employs the *Bildungsroman* technique effectively.

Balram comes to know about his purpose of life over a period of time with a remarkable change by experiencing the excruciating pains as a dishwasher and chauffeur with his fellow beings as well as with the upper caste community. Adiga suggests that anything is possible in India to become a rich man. The system of modern India is outmoded in view of achieving certain things in a fair way.

However, the novelist adopts a different technique to shape the character, who changes his personality. Having begun with a murder, the main character, belonging to a low caste, goes on to be a successful entrepreneur. Adiga is criticised for having taken up the tragic element of murdering the owner to uplift the main character. It is suggested that he could have chosen other choices.

The identity crisis in Balram generates great aspirations. He aspires for social recognition. He struggles for a good career. He is humiliated in his search for job: "Are you from a top caste or bottom caste, boy?" (64) Adiga is critical of upper caste Indians, who have a different attitude to the low caste when it comes to offering jobs. However, the hurdles, humiliation and struggles on the part of Balram help him acquire identity and self-confidence: "Once I was driver to a master, but now I am master of drivers. I don't treat them like servants-I don't slap, or bully, or mock anyone. I don't insult any of them by calling them my "family," either. There are my employees; I am their boss that's all. I make them sign a contract and I sign it too" (259).

Balram withstands all sorts of hurdles to get free from the social and political oppression. He assumes a different personality to become a successful entrepreneur. However, the cultural identity in Laxmangargh and the metropolitan backdrop shape him into a skilful person. When Balram becomes a successful person, he takes care of his own employees in a better way unlike what he had experienced with his erstwhile master who suppressed. He creates conducive atmosphere among the employees.

Balram discusses poetry with a bookseller and shares the verse "You were looking for the key for years/But the door was always open" (253). He often sits in the car, in the pose of Buddha while waiting for his master. He displays neither the poise nor the justification to his final action of the murder of his master. Balram undergoes mental rage because of this situation.

He plans a trip to the national zoo with his nephew Dharam. He comes to the enclosure with tall bamboo bars, where a white tiger is housed: "Not any kind of tiger. The creature that was born only once in every generation in the jungle" (276). The eye of contact that Balram makes with the white tiger is like a moment of epiphany. He faints at the revelation.

Later when Dharam writes a letter to his granny, Balram is determined to tell her the whole truth about what happened at the zoo. His grandmother tells of Balram raving again and again for no longer being able to live in a cage: "They turned to me and said, 'your uncle is raving- he's saying goodbye to his grandmother. He must think he's going to die,' Uncle's eyes were open now. Are you all right, Uncle?' I asked. He took my hand and he said, 'I am sorry, I am sorry, I am sorry.' I asked, "Sorry for what?" (278).

By implication, it may be understood that India is a jungle as Adiga views it; Balram is the white tiger, who has broken free from the cage. Ironically, the moral dilemma of Balram, in reaching this state of mind is not appreciated by the readers. The reader may understand the nature of Balram's existence to a great extent. The readers may empathise with his character.

However, the readers may not understand or appreciate the choice made by Balram. Balram's claims of entrepreneur skills and kindness for his employees, towards the end of the novel, appear hollow. The image of the white tiger is evoked by Balram too: "Take the money, and start a school- an English-language school- for poor children in Bangalore. A school where you won't be allowed to corrupt anyone's head with prayers and stories about God or Gandhi-nothing but the facts of life for these kids" (319-20).

IV

An ironic tone marks the narrative. The novel depicts the story of a talented man belonging to a low caste. Adiga shows how the character grows from childhood to adulthood. According to Bhikhu Parekh, "in any society, human beings are involved in a series of roles in terms of which they are identified. This practice gives rise to a great number of identifications based on traits, beliefs, etc" (Parekh 15).

The novel portrays the quest for identity, which is central in the novel. The caste-based discrimination hinders the growth of the individuals. According to Nathaniel Branden: "Individualism is at once an ethical-psychological concept and an ethical-political one. As an ethical-psychological concept, individualism holds that a human being should think and judge independently, respecting nothing more than the sovereignty of his or her mind; thus, it is intimately connected with the concept of autonomy.(Branden web) Adiga describes individualism in terms of one's rights to break free from the social restrictions. Adiga is critical of the Indian administrative system. In spite of more than half a century of the Independence governance, the administrative system is no longer effective and efficient towards the common man.

Thus, an attempt has been made in this chapter to examine Adiga's *The White Tiger* with a thrust on the social aspect. It has been argued that Adiga represents through the novel the modern India in the social contexts of feudal oppression, casteism and dalit suppression. The chapter has also examined the individual's growth and the use of the *Bildungsroman* in portraying the subjectivity. The novel has been interpreted with Lisa Lau's concept of 're-Orientalism.' Adiga, as against the Orientalist Western intelligentsia, critiques the socio-economic and political policies of the rulers of modern India, which have failed the aspirations of the people in the Independent country.

Works Cited

Aptor, A.J. "Human Actions and the theory of Psychological Reversals." *Aspects of Consciousness.* Ed. G. Underwood and R. Stevens. *Psychological Issues* Vol.1. London: Academic Press, 1979. Print.

Allport, G.W. "The Comparison of Political attitudes."*American Journal of Sociology* XXXV (1929). Print.

Bhikhu, Parekh. *A New Politics of Identity*. London: Palgrave Macmillan, 2008. Print.

Copley, Jennifer. "Behavioural Traits of Psychopaths." July 30, 2008. Web.

Erik H, Erikson. "Identity and the life cycle: Selected Papers." *Psychological Issues* 1.1959. Print.

—. "Identity and the life cycle: Selected Papers," *Psychological Issues*. 1. 1959. Print.

Siegesmund, Richard. "Subjectivity." *The Sage Encyclopedia of Qualitative Research Methods*., 2008. Sage Publications. 30April 2010.<http://www.sage-ereference.com/research/Article n438.html.>

Garrick, Jacqueline and Williams, Mary Beth. *Trauma treatment Techniques: Innovative Trends*. England: Haworth Maltreatment and Trauma Press, 2005. Print.

Higgins, Charlotte. "Out of the Darkness: Adiga's White Tiger rides to Booker Victory against the odds." *The Guardian*. 14 Octo. 2008. Web.

—. "Out of the Darkness: Adiga's White Tiger rides to Booker victory against the odds." *The Guardian*. 14 October 2008. Web.

Hall, C.S. and Lindzey, G. *Theories of Personality*. New York: John Wily, 1964. Print.

Jean, Drez and Sen, Amatya. "Democratic Practice and Social Inequality in India." *Journal of Asian and African Studies*, Vol. 37 No. 2 (2002). Print.

Kapur, Akash. "Review" *New York Times*, Nov. 7, 2008. Web.

Kumar, Amitava. "On Adiga's *The White Tiger*. *The Hindu*, Nov. 2, 2008. New Delhi. Print.

Lau, Lisa. "Reorientalism: The Perpetration and Development of Or ientalism and Orientalists" In *Modern Asian Studies*. England: CUP, 2007. Print.

Lima, Maria Helana. "Decolonising Genre: Jamaica Kincaid and the *Bildungsroman*." *Genre*, 26 winter (1993). Print.

Moretti, Franco. *The Way of the World*: The Bildungsroman in European Culture. London: Verso, 1999.Print.

Mukherjee, Meenakshi. *Twice Born Fiction*. Delhi: Pencraft International, 2001. Print.

—. *Twice-born Fiction*. Delhi: Pencraft International, 2001. Print.

Marianne, Hirsch. "The Novel of Formation as Genre: Between Great expectations and Los illusions", *Genre* 12 (3) (1979). Print.

Michael, Kilburn. "Glossary of Key Terms in the Work of Gayatri Chakravorty Spivak." Ariel 23:3 (July 1992). http://www.english.emory.edu/Bahri/Glossary.htmlWeb.

Nandy, Ashis. *The Intimate Enemy*: Loss and Recovery of Self under Colonialism. New Delhi: OUP, 2007. Print.

—. *The Intimate Enemy*: Loss and Recovery of Self under Colonialism. New Delhi: OUP, 2007. Print.

—. *The Intimate Enemy*: Loss and Recovery of Self under Colonialism. New Delhi: OUP, 2007. Print.

Prasannarajan, S. "Books: Driving out of Darkness" *India Today,* April 17, 2008. Print.

Raaju, Neelam. "Any tears for the Aam Aadmi?" *Sunday Times of India*. October 19, 2008. Web.

Slaughter, Joseph. *Human Rights. Inc.* New York: Fordham UP. 2008. Print.

The Oxford English Dictionary, Britain: OUP, Vol. V, 1961. Print.

http://freedomkeys.com/collectivism.htm June 21/2015.

http://www.complete-review.com/reviews/india/adigaa.htm 17April.2008.

Chapter - 8

Conclusion: Globalisation of Indian English Novel

The present study "The Booker and the post-colonial: Indian Award Winning Novels" has been an attempt to examine Indian Booker Prize novelists' engagement with the representation of India in the post-colonial context. Though the novelists' engagement with India is not new, there has been a perceivable difference in the representation of India between the novelists belonging to the first generation and the post-eighties period. The first generation novelists, led by the troika—R.K. Narayan, Mulk Raj Anand and Raja Rao—were preoccupied with the question of nationalism in tune with the backdrop of the freedom movement, each one from different perspective: Narayan preoccupied with the Indian ethos, Anand with the social construct and Raja Rao with the spiritual focus. Then second generation Indian English novelists continued with the tradition laid down by the originators of the genre; they could not come out of the magic spell of the troika, and therefore continued the tradition set by their unacknowledged mentor writers.

It is interesting to note that the first as well as the second generation Indian English novelists obviously connived at some of the most burning issues rocking the nation. To name a few, caste, religion, poverty, the anachronic character of social institutions such as marriage and family did not attract the attention of the first and the second generation novelists, although Anand is an exception in representing caste and poverty. While Raja Rao is explicit in Hindu revivalist ideology, writers like Narayan not only avoided being explicit, but in fact they have been oblique when it came to the question of caste. Narayan is especially evasive about this aspect and cautious in even naming his characters. In this respect, it may thus be said that the Indian English novel of the early period is urban in character and evasive about matters of ideology and commitment.

The contemporaries of the Indian English novelists in the rest of the post-colonial countries contrarily have been affirmative of representing caste, identity, gender and other socio-political constructs. The post-colonial novel in the rest of the world is rather ideological and political. The African and Latin-American novels, for instance, are antithetical to the early Indian English novel in respect of representation, nationalism and protest.

When it comes to nationalism and representation, the early Indian English novel is antithetical to the bhasha novel in India. The novel in Hindi, Bengali, Malayalam, Telugu and other Indian languages may be characterised as reformative, nationalistic, social and political. In this respect, the Indian novel in the regional languages has been truly representative of India unlike the early Indian English novel.

However, the character of the Indian English novel underwent an important change with the emergence of the post-modernist novelists. 1981 being the landmark year, Salman Rushdie effected the much desired epochal shift in the course of the Indian English novel. The epochal shift in the problematisation of India as a theme started with Rushdie's most influential novel *Midnight's Children* which became a benchmark for the Indian novelists in English both because of the intrinsic qualities of the work and the Booker Prize that it had won for its author. The awarding of the Booker prize to the novel earned equal significance to the Booker Prize itself.

A host of the recent Indian English novelists that include Upamanyu Chatterjee, Amitav Ghosh, Bharati Mukherjee, Gita Hariharan, John Master, Shashi Deshpande, Ruskin Bond, Arun Joshi, Arundhati Roy, Shiv K. Kumar, R.R. Menon, Ann Bhalla, Kiran Desai, Aravind Adiga, among others, touched upon some of the fundamental aspects of India, which had essentially been ignored or just glossed over by the early English novelists. It is in this respect that the recent Indian English novel differs in typology from its counterpart of the early period. The entire gamut of the recent Indian English novel may be said to have been influenced by the institution of the Booker Prize both in shaping the themes and concerns and styles and techniques.

The third chapter therefore has been devoted to the delineation of the origin, popularity, controversies and politics that surrounded the Booker Prize. The chapter examines the shift in the nature of the patronage system with a greater emphasis now on public sponsorship, besides exploring how the critics have given their opinion on the Booker Prize and its consequences on the reception of the novels. The sponsoring of the Prize, it has been argued, influences the critics' opinion leading to the creation of the hype surrounding the novel. The chapter concludes with an argument that the literary prizes legitimise mechanisms that have symbolic as well as material effects on the literary production.

The subsequent four chapters have been devoted to the representation of India by examining the four Indian Booker Prize winning novels: Salman Rushdie's *The Midnight's Children*, Arundhati Roy's *The God of Small Things*, Kiran Desai's *The Inheritance of Loss* and Aravind Adiga's *The White Tiger.* The novelists creatively focused in their respective novels on the social, political, economic and historical aspects of India. The first Indian Booker Prize winning novel *Midnight's Children* explores the pre-independence and post-independence Indian history. Rushdie is successful in terms of showing the historical events in the novel. The tragic incident of the Jallianwallah Bagh massacre, the Partition and the excesses of the National Emergency are depicted critically in the novel. Rushdie depicts the recent Indian history through the 'midnight's children.' Of the 1001 children, 420 children die. The number alludes to *Shree 420*, a film which has a perceivable influence on Rushdie. It is as if the moment of India's independence was a moment of promise for humanity, signified by the 'Midnight's Children Council' as a group capable of profound understanding. Nehru's vision of building the modern India had been shattered with the gruesome incidents that followed the Independence.

Rushdie explores another gruesome incident of 1970-78 encompassing the sub-partition of Pakistan bringing into being yet another country, Bangladesh. The novel shows the ways in which history is recorded and the techniques through which the individual historiographer understands his relationship to his material. *Midnight's Children* is a historical novel because it is consistent with the criteria of historical veracity that it sets within itself.

Arundhati Roy's exploration of the social history of India with reference to the oppression of the untouchables as well as gender issues is another form of writing India, and this aspect is examined in the fourth chapter. It has been argued in the chapter that Roy seeks to project the south Indian rural family focusing on the socio-cultural specificities of the region thereby marking another epochal shift in foregrounding the local against the global. The novel is not based on the witnessed truth but works as a fictive creation of a society where higher castes suppress the lower castes. The narration delineates the accurate repression of intra-caste relations. The novel also explores the events and experiences of the novelist's birth place where the communists and the upper class Syrian Christian families' domination of the social space are sharply critiqued. The novel portrays the social history of the modern India incisively, besides depicting objectionable aspects of patriarchy.

Kiran Desai's *The Inheritance of Loss* has been interpreted as a novel dealing with Indian history vis-à-vis globalisation. Set partly in New York and partly in the Gorkhaland region in India, the novel presents how history exerts adverse influence on the life of the common people. The impact has been portrayed to be transmitting from one generation to the next. The novel explores the aspect of the introduction of the Western element into India during the colonial period, and how the same is repeated with the Americanisation of India in the last decades of the twentieth century. Desai juxtaposes the history of the Gorkhaland movement that affected West Bengal for several years irrevocably changing the political map of the Darjeeling hill region. The novel is critical of the barbarity of the state police and the inhuman violence perpetuated by the insurgents. The novel highlights the effects of the movement on the people of Kalimpong, and how they reacted to it. The novel in brief portrays the victims and the survivors.

Aravind Adiga's *The White Tiger* explores the modern India and its economic and political conditions, tracing the growth through the main character from childhood to maturity. Having adopted the technique of the *Bildungsroman*, the novelist critically portrays the development of the main character. There are explicit illustrations of the gross malpractices in the Indian democracy. The novel could be read as the social criticism focusing on the country's poverty and misery. Besides, the novel portrays effectively, the religious, social and political conflicts. Adiga's nuanced observations of the current political system in India and its problems such as corruption in political system, judiciary, police and health among others, are sharp. The main character's progression through them from the India of darkness to the India of light has been examined in the chapter.

The four novelists selected for the study have made immense contribution to the formation of the sub-genre 'Recent Indian English Novel,' which became predominantly visible on the world literary scene. Their contribution lies in being global and local at the same time and in refusing to mimic the European poetics as well as Sanskrit poetics.

These four novelists, together with several others of the post-Rushdie generation, also contributed a great deal to the narrative technique of the Indian novel in English. Prior to Rushdie the narrative technique employed by Indian novelist in English was largely imitative and it hardly evidenced originality on the novelists' part. Although Mulk Raj Anand and Raja Rao strained to lend local colour by means of infusing their fictional narratives with Indian expressions they did not quite succeed in convincing the reading public that they evolved a distinctive narrative mode. Most often their experiments remained linguistic curiosities and did not inspire emulation by others. Their vocabulary too was very limited and their diction was not entirely appropriate in various contexts. Further they had difficulty in matching the English language with the Indian themes and this difficulty resulted in producing a comical effect when actually the intention was serious.

With Rushdie all this changed at one go. He inaugurated a new era not only in terms of the choice of subject matter of fictional works but also in terms of the narrative technique. His, and that of his successors, is a narrative technique that well matches the subject and often draws attention to itself. But for this new mode of writing Rushdie, Roy and the other Booker novelists would hardly gained the kind of attention they finally gained and they, as writers would have been hardly has great as they are today. Be means of this bold experimentation they elevated the Indian novel in English to the structure of world literature and secured its place on the world literary stage for all times to come. The winning of the Booker prize is only an official recognition accorded to their literary achievement. The Booker thus has a great symbolic value for not just these four novelists but for the entire gamut of the recent Indian fiction in English.

These four novelists, more specifically their Booker Prize winning novels, have already been studied by scholars from various angles. Especially Salman Rushdie's *Midnight's Children* and Arundhati Roy's *The God of Small Things* have been the objects of much critical analysis. The present study itself has endeavoured to map them and the two other booker novels as forming part of post-modern Indian English fiction which antithetical to the non-committed, 'secular,' colourless and odourless early Indian English fiction. But no amount of scholarship can ever exhaust all the critical possibilities of master works of fiction. As T.S. Eliot has famously said each generation has to interpret literary classics for itself. These novels too have to be further studied and interpreted and one does not need to wait for the generation to change. Knowledge multiplies these days so fast that it is possible, if one makes an honest attempt, to study and interpet these novels from ever new perspectives every year! The present study has been only a modest attempt and it does not at all claim to be exhaustive countless other possibilities of studying these novels obviously exist and it is for the future researchers to identify these possibilities and approach the novels with fresh insights gained from the expanding knowledge in various fields of scholarly pursuit.

Select Bibliography

Primary Sources

Rushdie, Salman. *Midnight's Children*. London: Jonathan Cape, 1981.

Roy, Arundhati. *The God of Small Things*. New Delhi: Penguin Books India, 2002.

Desai, Kiran. *The Inheritance of Loss*. New Delhi: Penguin, 2006.

Adiga, Aravind. *The White Tiger.* New Delhi: Harper Collins, 2008.

Secondary Sources

I. Books

Achebe, C. *Morning Yet on Creation Day*. New York: Anchor Press, 1975.

Adas, M. *Machines as the Measure of Men. Ithaca*. New York: Cornell University Press, 1989.

Anderson, B. *Imagined Communities: Reflections on the Origin and Spread of Nationalism*. New York: Verso, 1991.

Appadurai, A. *Modernity at Large: Cultural Dimensions of Globalisation*. London: University of Minnesota Press, 1996.

Arnold, D. *Colonizing the Body: State Medicine and Epidemic Disease in Nineteenth Century India*. Berkley: University of California Press,1993.

Achebe, Chinua. *Morning Yet On Creation Day.* London: Heinemann, 1975.

Ashcroft, Bill, Gareth Griffiths, and Helen Tiffm. *The Empire Writes Back: Theory and Practice in Post-colonial Literature.* London: Routledge, 1998.

—. eds. *The Post-Colonial Studies Reader.* London: Routledge, 1995.

—. *Key Concepts in Post-Colonial Studies.* London: Routledge, 1998.

Awanoor, Kofi. *The Breast of the Earth.* London: Routledge, 1989.

Aslam, Nadeem. *Season of the Rain birds*. London: André Deutsch, 1993.

Ahuja, Ram. *Social Problems in India*. Jaipur: Rawat Publications, 2004.

Ashcroft, Bill. *Post Colonial Transformation.* London: Routledge, 2001.

Ambedkar, B.R. *What Congress and Gandhi Have Done to the Untouchables.* Mumbai: Thacker and Co., 1946.

Ambedkar, B.R. *The Untouchables: Who were they and why They became Untouchables?* New Delhi: Amrit, 1948.

—. *Who Were the Shudras? How They Came to be the Fourth Varna in the Indo-Aryan Society.* Mumbai: Thackers, 1970.

Alter, Joseph. *The Wrestler's Body: Identity and Ideology in North India.* Berkeley: U California P, 1992.

Barnes, Harry Elmer. *A History of Historical Writing.* 2nd rev ed. New York: Dover Publications, 1962.

Barraclough, Geoffrey. *Main Trends in History*. New York: Holmes and Meir, 1977.

Barthes, Roland. "Historical Discourse," *Structuralism:* A Reader Ed. Michael Lane. London: Jonathan Cape, 1970.

Bhabha, Homi. "Introduction: Location of Culture." *The Location of Culture,* London: Routledge, 1994.

Bhaskaran, Suparma. *Made in India: Decolonisations, Queer Sexualities, transnational Projects.* London: Palgrave-Macmillan, 2004.

Brah, Avtar. *Cartographies of Diaspora: Contesting identities.* London and New York: Routledge, 1997.

Brennan, Timothy. *Salman Rushdie and the Third World: Myths of the Nation.* New York: St. Martin Press, 1989.

Bloom, Howard. *Where Shall Wisdom Be Found?* USA: Riverhead Books, 2004.

Bakthin, Michael. *Rabelais and His World.* Trans. Hellene Iswosky. Bloomington: Indiana UP, 1984.

Banham, Martin. "On Being Squelched in the Spittle of an Alien Race." *Wole Soyinka an Appraisal.* Ed. Adewale Maja Pearce. London: Heinemann, 1994: 128-132.

—. Introduction *The Cambridge Guide to African and Caribbean Theatre.* Ed. Martin Banharn, Erril Hill and George Wood Cambridge: Cambridge UP, 1994.

Banks, Thomas. "Wole Soyinka." *Critical Survey of Drama. English Language Series. Authors Shaw-Z.* Ed. Frank. N. Magill. New Jersey: Saleem, 1986: 1845-1857.

—. "Wole Soyinka". *Encyclopedia of Critics on Criticism.* Ed. Chris Murray. 2 Vols. London: Fitzroy Dearborn, 1999. 1040-1055.

Barry, Peter. *Beginning Theory: An Introduction to Literary and Cultural Theory.* Manchester: Manchester UP, 1995.

Beier, Ulli. *A Year of Sacred Festival in Our Yoruba Town.* Lagos: Nigeria Magazine, 1959.

Bhaba, Homi K. "Of Mimicry and Man: The Ambivalence of Colonial Discourse". *The Location of Culture.* London: Routledge, 1994.

—. "Post-colonial Criticism." *The Location of Culture.* London: Routledge, 1994.

Bharnbani, Meenu. "Thematic Perspectives of Culture in Wole Soyinka's *Death and the King's Horseman.*" *Contesting Post colonialism.* Ed. Jasbir Jain and Veena Singh. New Delhi: Rawat, 2000: 203-206.

Boehmer, Elleke. *Colonial and Postcolonial Literature: Migrant Metaphors.* Oxford: Oxford UP, 1995.

Booth, Jarnes. *Writers and Politics in Nigeria.* London: Hodder, 1981.

Benson, Eugene and L.W. Conolly (eds). *Encyclopaedia of Post-Colonial Literature.*

Brandist, Craig. *Carnival Culture and the Soviet Modernist Novel.* London: Macmillan, 1996.

Chakrabarty, Dipesh. *Habitations of Modernity.* New Delhi: Permanent Black, 2002.

Carey, Peter. *Bliss.* New York: Vintage, 1996.

—.*Illywhacker.* New York: Vintage, 1996.

Chaudhuri, Nirad C. *The Autobiography of an Unknown Indian.* London: Macmillan, 1951.

—.*Thy Hand, Great Anarch: India 1921-1952.* London: Chatto and Windus, 1987.

Chandra, Vikram. *Red Earth and Pouring Rain.* London: Faber, 1995.

—.*Love and Longing in Bombay.* London: Faber, 1997.

—.*Sacred Games.* London: Faber, 2006.

Chaudhuri, Amit. *A Strange and Sublime Address.* London: Heinemann, 1991.

Chaudhuri, Nirad C. *The Autobiography of an Unknown Indian.* London: Macmillan, 1951.

Collingwood, R G. *The Idea of History.* USA: Oxford Paperbacks, 1971.

Crane, Ralph J. *Inventing India: A History of India in English-Language Fiction.* London: Macmillan, 1992.

Chandra, Sanehlata. *Marginal Communities and Social Development.* New Delhi: Kanisha Publications, 1998.

Chatterji, Partha. *The Nation and its Fragments.* Delhi: OUP, 1992.

Conrad, J. *Heart of Darkness.* Harmondsworth: Penguin, 1975.

Cook, David. *African Literature. A Critical Review.* London: Longman, 1978.

Campbell, Joseph. "The Historical Development of Mythology." *Myth and Myth Making.* Ed. Henry A. Murray Boston: Beacon, 1960: 19-45.

Crow, Brian, and Chris Banfield. *An Introduction to Post-colonial Theatre.* Cambridge: Cambridge UP, 1996.

Cesare, Airne. *Discourse on Colonialism.* Trans. Joan Penkham. New York: Monthly Review, 1972.

Clark, Katerine and Holquist, Michael. *Michael Bakthin.* Cambridge: Harvard UP, 1984.

David, Kingsley. *Human Society.* New Delhi: Surjeet Publications, 1995.

Dhar, T.N. *History-Fiction Interface in Indian English Novel.* New Delhi: Prestige, 1999.

Das, Bijay Kumar. *Twentieth Century Literary Criticism.* New Delhi: Atlantic Publishers, 1998.

Davidar, David. *The House of Blue Mangoes*. New Delhi: Penguin India, 2002.

—.*The Solitude of Emperors*. London: Weidenfeld and Nicolson, 2007.

Edgar, David. "The Migrant's Vision." *New Left Review*. 1981.

Fleishman, Avrom. *The English Historical Novel: Walter Scott to Virginia Woolf*. Baltimore: The John Hopkins Press, 1971.

Fanon, Frantz. *The Wretched of the Earth.* London: Penguin, 1967.

Ghosh, Amitav. *The Circle of Reason*. London: Hamish Hamilton, 1986.

—.*The Shadow Lines*. New Delhi: Ravi Dayal, 1988.

Gonzalez, Madelena. *Fiction after the Fatwa: Salman Rushdie and the Charm of Catastrophe.* Amsterdam: Rodopi, 2005.

Gandhi, Leela. *Postcolonial Theory: A Critical Introduction*. New Delhi: OUP, 2002.

Guha, Ranajit. *Subaltern Studies II: Writing on South Asian History and Society.* New Delhi: OUP, 1983.

Gilbert, Helen and Joanne, Tompkins. *Postcolonial Drama, Theory, Practice, Politics.* London: Routledge, 1996.

Griffiths, Gareth and David Moody. "Of Mm and Missionaries; Soyinka and the Survival of Universalism in Post colonial Literary Theory." *After Europe: Critical Theory and Post Colonial Writing.* Ed. Stephen Slemon and Helen Tiffin. Sidney: Dangaroo,1989.

Gilman, S. *Difference and Pathology: Stereotypes of Sexuality, Race and Madness.* London: Cornell University Press, 1985.

Gramsci, A. *Selections from the Prison Notebooks.* Q. Hoare and G.N. Smith (eds) London: Lawrence and Wishart, 1971.

Gilroy, Paul. *The Black Atlantic: Modernity and Double Consciousness.* Cambridge: Harvard UP, 1993.

Huggan, Graham. *Peter Carey*. Melbourne: OUP, 1996.

—.*The Postcolonial Exotic: Marketing and Margins:* London and NY: Routledge, 2001.

Hariharan, Githa. *The Ghosts of Vasu Master*. New Delhi: Penguin India, 1994.

Hume, David. *A Treatise of Human Nature.* Mineola, New York: Dover Publications, Inc. 2003.

Hutchinson, Linda. *The Poetics of Postmodernism: History, Theory and Fiction.* London: Routledge, 1998.

—.*The Reluctant Fundamentalist*. New York: Penguin, 2007.

Hanif, Mohammed. *A Case of Exploding Mangoes*. London: Random House, 2008.

Iyenger, Srinivas K.R. *The Indian Writing in English.* New Delhi: Sterling Publications India, 2011.

Jackson, Rosemary. *Fantasy: The Literature of Subversion.* London: Routledge, 1981.

Joyce, James. *A Portrait of the Artist as a Young Man.* Delhi: Surjeet Publications, 1991.

Khilnani, Sunil. *The Idea of India*. New York: Farrar, 1997.

Kinslay, David. *Hindu Goddessess*. London: Univ. of California Press, 1988.

Lee, Alison. 'Realism and Power,' *Postmodern British Fiction.* London and New York: Routledge, 1990.

Lerner, Laurence. *The Frontiers of Literature*. Oxford: Basil Blackwell, 1988.

Mistry, Rohinton. *Such a Long Journey*. London: Faber, 1991.

—.*A Fine Balance*. London : Faber, 1996.

Mukharjee, Meenakshi. *Perishable Empire*: Essays on Indian Writing in English. New Delhi: OUP, 2000.

—.*The Twice Born Fiction: Themes and Techniques of the Indian Novel in English*. New Delhi: Heinemann Educational Books, 1971.

Moffit, Michael. *An Untouchable Community in South India.* Princeton, N. J.: Princeton UP, 1979.

Maragareta, Peterson. *Unending Metamorpheses.* Lund: Student Literature, 1996.

Mathew, Jojo. *Wizard Current Affairs 2008.* 6th (ed) Delhi: Carrier Classics, 2008.

Nayar, Pramod. K. *Postcolonial Literature: An Introduction,* New Delhi: Pearson Publication, 2008.

—.*English Writing in India, 1600-1920: Colonizing Aesthetics.* New Delhi: Routledge, 2007.

Naik, M.K. "A Life of Fragments": The Fate of Identity in *Midnight's Children.*" in *Studies in Indian English Literature.* New Delhi: Sterling Publishers, 1987.

Parch, Pradeep R. "Krishna: Myth or Reality"? Bombay: Jaico Publishing House, 1980.

Rao, Raja. *Kanthapura*. London: G. Allen and Unwin, 1938.

—.*The Serpent and the Rope*. London: John Murray, 1960.

Said, Edward W. *Orientalism.* London: Penguin, 1985.

—.*Culture and Imperialism.* London: Chatto, 1993.

Said, Edward. *The World, The Text and the Critic.* Cambridge: Harvard UP, 1983.

Sartre, Jean Paul. *Colonialism and Neo-colonialism.* London: Routledge, 2001.

Sewall, Richard B. *The Vision of Tragedy.* London: Yale UP, 1980.

Sharma, Meenakshi. *Postcolonial Indian Writing. Between Co-option and Resistance.* Delhi: Rawat, 2003.

Sharpe, Jenny. *Allegories of Empire: The Figure of Woman in the Colonial Text.* Minneapolis: Minnesota UP, 1994.

Singh, Pramod Kumar. *Indian Fiction in English*. New Delhi: Atlantic Publishers, 2001.

Spivak, Gayatri Chakravorty. 'Can the Subaltern Speak?' *Colonial Discourse/Post-Colonial Theory*. New York: CUP, 1994.

Stanley, Wolport. *A New History of India*. London: OUP, 1982.

Suleri, Sara. *The Rhetoric of English India.* Chicago: U. Chicago Press, 1992.

Singh, K.S. *The Schedule Castes: The People of India. National Series*. Vol. 2 of the Anthropological Survey of India. Delhi: OUP, 1993.

Shakespeare, Williams. *Macbeth.* New Delhi: Peacock Books, 2007. Act V Sc I.

Sterba, James P. *Three Challenges to Ethics*. OUP: New York, 2001.

Sassen, Saskia. *Globalisation and its Discontents.* New York: The New Press, 1998.

Tharoor, Sashi. *The Great Indian Novel.* New Delhi: Penguin India, 1989.

Thing' O, NgugiWa. *Writers and Politics.* London: Heinemann, 1981.

—.*Homecoming: Essays on African and Carribbean Literature, Culture and Politics.* London: Heinemann, 1972.

—.*Moving the Centre: The Struggle for Cultural Freedoms.* London: Heinemann, 1993.

Uma, Parameshwaran. *A Study of Representative Indo-English Novelists*. New Delhi: Vikas Pub. House, 1976.

Viswanathan, Gauri. *Masks of Conquest: Literary Study and British Rule in India.* Delhi: OUP, 1998.

Walsh, W. H. *An Introduction to Philosophy of History*. London: Hutchinson, 1951.

Warder, A.K. *An Introduction to Indian Historiography*. Bombay: Popular Prakashan, 1972.

Walsh, William. *Common Wealth Literature*. London: OUP, 1973.

Young, Robert. *Colonial Desire: Hybridity in Theory, Culture and Race,* London and New York: Routledge, 1995.

...*Postcolonialism: An Historical Introduction*. Oxford: Blackwell, 2001.

II. Anthologies

Alter, Stephen and Wimal Dissanayake, eds. *The Penguin Book of Modern Indian Short Stories*. New Delhi: Penguin India, 1989.

Anand, Mulk Raj and Zelliot Eleanor, eds. *An Anthology of Dalit Literature*. New Delhi: Gyan Publishing House, 1992.

Banerjee, Ashutosh. "Narrative technique in *Midnight's Children*." Three Contemporary Novelists. Ed. R.K. Dhawan. New Delhi: Classical Publishing Company, 1985: 196-198.

Chaudhuri, Amit. *The Picador Book of Modern Indian Literature*. London: Picador, 2002.

Chaudari, Nirad C. *The Autobiography of an Unknown Indian*. New York: New York Review of Books, 2001.

Chandra, N.D.R. "Multiplicity of feminine Gender Identity in *The God of Small Things. Indian Women Novelists in English*. Ed. Jaydipsinh Dodiya. Atlantic Publisher, 2006:150-162.

Achebe, Chinua. 'The Novelist as Teacher.' *Commonwealth Literature: Unity and Diversity in a Commonwealth*. Ed. John Press. Oxford: Heinemann, 1965: 201- 205.

—."Colonialist Criticism." *The Post-colonial Studies Reader.*

Ed. Bill Ashcroft, Gareth Griffiths and Helen Tiffm. London: Routledge, 1995: 57-61.

Dangle, Arjun, ed. *The Poisoned Bread: Translation from Modern Dalit Literature*. Hyderabad: Orient Longman, 1992.

Daruwalla, Keki, ed. *Two Decades of Indian Poetry 1960-1980*. Delhi: Vikas Publishing, 1980.

De Souza, Eunice, ed. *Nine Indian Women Poets: An Anthology*. Delhi: OUP, 1997.

Dharwadker, Vinay and A.K. Ramanujan, eds. *The Oxford Anthology of Modern Indian Poetry*. Delhi: OUP, 1994.

Eagleton, Mary, ed. *Feminist Literary Theory: A Reader*. New York: Basil Blackwell, 1986.

Ezekiel, Nissim and Meenakshi Mukherjee, eds. *Another India: an Anthology of Contemporary Indian Fiction and Poetry*. Delhi: Penguin India, 1989.

Hale, J.R., ed. *The Evolution of British Historiography*. London: Macmillan, 1967.

Jussawalla, Adil, Ed. *New Writing in India*. Delhi: Penguin, 1974.

James, Henry. “The Art of Fiction,” *The Theory of the American Novel,* ed. George Perkins (U.S.A.: Holt, Rhinehart and Winston, 1970): 178.

John, Clement Ball. “Pessoptimism: Satire and the manippean Grotesque in Rushdie’s *Midnight’s Children and Salman Rushdie: New critical Insights.* Ed. Rajeshwar Mittapalli and Joel Kuortti. Atlantic Publisher: New Delhi (2003): 87-114.

Kohli, Devindra. Ed. *Indian Writers at work* (transcript of interviews). Delhi: BR Publishing, 1991.

Lodge, David. “The Novelist at the Cross Roads,” *The Novel Today* ed. Malcolm Bradbury (Great Britain: Pontana, (1977): 85-93.

Mehrotra, Arvind Krishna. Ed. *The Oxford Anthology of Twelve Modern Indian Poets*. New Delhi: OUP, 1992.

Mishra, Vijay. “The Texts of Mother India.” *After Europe.* Ed. Stephen Slemon and Helen Tiffin. Sydney: Dangaroo Press, (1989): 119-37.

Misra, Viya. “New Lamps for Old Diaspora Colonial Discourse and Post-Colonial Theory: A Reader.” Ed. Patrick Williams and Laura Charisma. New York: Harvester Wheatsheaf, 1994. 399-408.

Pandey, Surya Nath, ed. *Writing in a Post-Colonial Space.* Atlantic Publishers, Delhi: 1999, 23-28.

Pathak, R.S. “History and the individual in the novels of Rushdie.” *Three Contemporary Novelists*. Ed. R.K. Dhawan. New Delhi: Classical, 1985, 217.

Rushdie, Salman and Elizabeth West. Eds. *The Vintage Book of Indian Writing*. London: Vintage, 1997, 67-72.

Raghavendra Rao, K. “The Novel as History as ‘Chunty’: Unriddling Salman Rushdie’s *Midnight’s Children.” Perspectives of Indian Fiction in English.* Ed. M.K. Naik. New Delhi: Abhinav, 1985, 157-61.

Tharu, Susie and K. Lalita. Eds. *Women Writing in India*. 2 Vols. Delhi: OUP, 1995.

Walsh, William. “India and the Novel.” *The New Pelican Guide to English Literature.* Ed. Boris Ford. Middlesex: Penguin Books, 1983, 13-22.

III. Articles

Ali, Tariq. *Midnight's Children* by Salman Rushdie. *New Left Review,* 136 (1982):87-95.

Ahmed, Aizaz. "Reading Arundhati Roy politically" *Frontline*, August 8, (1997):103-108.

Avishai, Margalit. "Decent Equality and Freedom: A Postscripts." *Social Research* 64.1 (Sep.1997): 147.

Agarwal, Ramlal. *The God of Small Things. World Literature Today* 72.1 (Winter 1998): 208-209.

Ajayan, C. "A Segment of Existence: Arundhati Roy's *The God of Small Things*." *Journal of Literature and Aesthetics* 5.2 (Jul-Dec 1997): 97-99.

Bhabha, Homi. "Signs Taken For Wonders: Questions of Ambivalence and Authority under a Tree outside Delhi, May 1817." *Critical Inquiry* 12.1 (1985):144-65.

Barbuddhe, Sathis. "*Midnight's Children*: A Blend of Autobiography, History and Fantasy" *The Common Wealth Review* Vol. xviii, No. 2 (2009): 67-76.

Bhaya Nair, Rukmuni. "Text and pre-Text: History as Gossip in Rushdie's Novels." *Economic and Political Weekly* 6 (May 1989): 994-1000.

Booker, M. Keith. "Beauty and the Beast: Dualism as despotism in the Fiction of Salman Rushdie." *ELH* 57 (1990): 977-97.

Bhaskaran, Subhadra. "The Sweetest song that sings of the saddest Tale: An Exposition of *The God of Small Things*." *Ariel* 21.2 (Jan. 1997): 19-29.

Bose, Brinda. "In Desire and in Death: Eroticism as politics in Arundhati Roy's *The God of Small Things. Ariel* 29. 2 (April 1998): 59-72.

Bhushan, Ravi. "Indian English Novel: A Historical Perspective and Problems." *The Common Wealth Review* 15.13 (2002): 42-48.

Chakrabarthi, Santhosh. "Myth and reality: Arundhati Roy's Use of language in *The God of Small Things. The Quest.* 16.1 (June 2002): 9-16.

Borges, Luis Jorge. "The Argentine Writer and Traditions: Labyrynths." *New Declarations* (1962): 179-190.

Balogun, F. Odun. "Wole Soyinka and the Literary Aesthetic of African Socialism." *Black American Literature Forum.* 22.3 (1988): 502-529.

Badijo, Diedre. "Unmasking of Gods: Of Egungirn and Demogogues in Three works of Wole Soyinka." *Black American Literature Forum* 22.4 (1988): 663-667.

Bowman, Mark Ralph. "Leaders and Left Overs." *Research in African Literatures* 14.1 (1983): 81-110.

Cielo G, Festino. "Still in Search of the Nation: A Reading of Aravind Adiga's *The White Tiger.*" *Indian Journal of Post-colonial Literatures* 10.2 (December 2010): 61-70.

Cielo G, Festino. "Indian Critics on Booker Prize." *The Times Literary Supplement* 5404 (Oct. 2006): 16.

Chen, Chunyen. "Betrayal of Form: The "Teeming" Narrative and the Allegorical Impulse in Rushdie's *Midnight's Children."* *The Journal of Common Wealth Literature,* 44.3 (2009): 143-161.

Cruz, Doreem D. "Configuring the Dynamics of Dispossession in Rohinton Mistry's *A Fine Balance* and Arundhati Roy's *The God of Small Things" New Zealand Journal of Asian Studies* 5.2 (2003): 56-76.

Chordiya, D.P. "Taking on the tone of Bombay Talkie: The Function of Bombay Cinema in Salman Rushdie's *Midnight's Children. ARIEL* 38.4 (2007): 97-121.

Dharkar, Rani. "Who's Afraid of the Big Bad Booker? The Making of Small Gods in our Times." Nanavati, U.M. Prafulla C. Kar ed. *Rethinking Indian Literatur.* Delhi: Pencraft (2000): 140-44.

Durix, Jean-Pierre. "Magic Realism in *Midnight's Children.*" *Commonwealth" Essays and studies* 8.1 (1985): 57-63.

Derrida, Jacques. "On Cosmopolitanism and Forgiveness." Trans. Mark Dooley and Michael Hughes, (2001): 25-60.

Dhar, T.N. "Micro-Macro Symbiosis: The Form of Salman Rushdie's *Midnight's Children." The Journal of Indian Writing in English* 13.1 (1985):16-23.

Dasenbrock, Reedway. "Wole Soyinka's Nobel Prize." *World Literature Today* 61.1 (1987): 5-9.

David, Mary T. *Wole Soyinka. A Quest for Renewal.* Madras: B.I., 1995.

Davis, Ann B. "Dramatic Theory of Wole Soyinka." *Critical Perspectives on Wole Soyinka.* Ed. James Gibbs. Washington DC: Three Continents, 1980: 147-157.

Dirlik, Arif. "The Postcolonial Aura: Third World Criticism in the Age of Global Capitalism." *Critical Inquiry* (1994): 333-338.

Dasan, A.S. "Questing for truth: History-Fiction Interface in the Recent Indian English Fiction." *Littcrit* 33.2 (Dec. 2007): 5-24.

Dhawan, R.K. Ed. *Indian Women Writers.* New Delhi: Prestige, (2000): 145-157.

Elizabeth, Outka. "Trauma and Temporal Hybridity in Arundhati Roy's *The God of Small Things. Contemporary Literature.* 52.1 (2001): 1-21.

Ferguson, Jesse Patrick. "Violent Dis-Placement: Natural and Human Violence in Kiran Desai's *The Inheritance of Loss." The Journal of Common Wealth Literature.* 44.2 (2009): 35-49.

George, Roshin. "Missippi and Meenachal: *The Adventures of Huckleberry Finn and The God of Small Things." The Quest* 15.2 (Dec 2001):17-21.

Ganguly, Rajat. "Poverty, Malgovernance and Ethnopolitical Mobilisation: Gorkha Nationalism and the Gorkhaland Agitation in India." *Nationalism and Ethnic Politics* 11(2005): 67-502.

Gurnah, Abdulrazak. "Themes and Structures in *Midnight's Children" The Cambridge Companion to Salman Rushdie,* ed. Abdulrazak Gurnah. (Cambridge: UK, 2007): 91-108.

Hill, Rowena. "Rushdie Vs Roy." *The Literary Criterion* 35.4 (2000): 78-82.

Hadley, Tessa. "Exotic to Whom" Rev of *The Inheritance of Loss. London Review Books* 28.19 (Oct. 2006): 8.

Huggan, Graham. "Prizing otherness': A Short History of the Booker," *Studies in the Novel* 29.3 (1997): 424.

Inamdar, F.A. "Predominant Issues in Kiran Desai's *The Inheritance of Loss" The Common Wealth Review* 18.2 (2009): 142-150.

Islam, Syed Manzural. "Writing the Postcolonial Event: Salman Rushdie August 15, 1947." *Textual Practice* 13.1 (1999): 128.

Isedore, Okpewho "The Mythic Essence" *The African Guardian* 30 October. 1986.

Iyengar, Sreenivasa K.R. "Soyinka's Latest Play." *Literary Half Yearly* 17.2 (1976): 3-17.

Izevbaye, D.S. "Language and Meaning in Soyinka's *The Road" African Literature Today* 8 (1988): 52-65.

Jacobs, Alan. "Wole Soyinka's Outrage: The Divided Soul of Nigerias Nobel Laureate." *Ariel* 128.4 (1997): 21-29.

Jeyifo, Biodiun. *Introduction to Six Plays by Wole Soyinka.* London: Methuen, 1984. (vi-xii).

—. "Interview with Wole Soyinka" *Transition* 42 (1973): 62-63.

Johnson, Chris. "Performance and Role Playing in Soyinka's *Madmen and Specialists." Journal of Commonwealth Literature,* XII. 2 (1977): 27-33.

Jones, Eldred Duro Sirni. "The Essential Soyinka." *Introduction to Nigerian Literature.* Ed. BruceKing. Ibadan: University of Lagos, 1977: 113-134.

—. "Wole Soyinka, Critical Approaches." *The Critical Evaluation of African Literature.* Ed. Edgar Wright. London: Heinemann, 1973: 51-72.

Jha, Surendra Narayan. "Dreams Re-Dreamed: A study of *The God Small Things*." Ed. Dhawan, R.K. *Indian Women Writers.* New Delhi: Prestige, (2000): 188-93.

Jayati, Ghosh. "Income Inequality in India." *People's Democracy.* February 17, 2008.

Jameson, Frederic. "Third world literature in the Era of Multinational Capitalism." *Social Text* 15 (1986):86-88.

Joanne Lipson, Feed. "The Ethics of identification: The Global Circulation of Traumatic Narrative in Silko's Ceremony and Roy's *The God of Small Things. Comparative Literature Studies* 48.2 (2011): 219-240.

Kurz, Helga Ramsay. "Does Saleem Really Miss the Spittoon? Script and Scriptlessness in *Midnight's* Children"*Journal of Common Wealth Literary Review.* 36.1 (2001): 127-143.

Kortenaar, Neil ten. "Postcolonial Emphasis: Salman Rushdie Gives the Finger Back to the Empire." *Contemporary Literature* 38.2 (1997): 247.

Kanganayakam, Chelvanayakam. "Myth and Febulosity in *Midnight's Children*" *Dalhousie Review* 67 (1987):86-98.

Keith Wilson, "Midnight's Children and Reader Responsibility," *Central quarterly* 26.3 (Autumn 1984): 23-28.

Kulkarni, Prahlad A., Book Review of Arundhati Roy's *The God of Small Things*, *Critical Practice* 4.1 January. (1999): 45-51.

Kaur, Tejinder. "Problematizing Issues about Home, Homeland, Diaspora and Belongingness in Transnational and National Lands: A Study of Kiran Desai's *The Inheritance of Loss." The Common Wealth Review* Xviii. 2 (2009): 129-140.

Katrak, Kethu H. *Wole Soyinka and Modern Tragedy. A Study of Dramatic Theory and Practice.* West Port: Greenwood, 1986.

—."Theory and Social Responsibility in Soyinka's Essays." *Black American Literature Forum* 22.3 (1988): 489-501.

Kildhall, Karen A. "Edward Said *Encyclopaedia of Critics on Criticism.* Ed. Chris Murray. 2 Vols. London: Fitzroy Dearborn, (1999): 971-973.

King Bruce. 1ntroduction: *Introduction to Nigerian Literature* Ed. Bruce King. Lagos: Evans, 1971. 1-11.

Kriegar, Murray. *The Tragic Vision. The Confrontation of Extremity.* London: Johns Hopkins UP, 1973.

Kapoor, Mini. "Of Longing and Belonging." *The Inheritance of Loss*, Biblio*: A Review of Books* 9.374 (Mar- Apri. 2006): 8.

Kala, Awind. "Your caste is your Life." *Scholastic Update* (Teacher's edition), 11, Apr. 1997: 129-31.

Lutz, J. "Commodity fetishism, Patriarchal repression, and Psychic Deprivation in Arundhati Roy's *The God of Small Things*" *Mosaic* 43.3 (2009): 57-74.

Larson, Charles R. "Wole Soyinka, The Wounds of War." *Nation* (5 Nov 1973): 470-482.

—. "Wole Soyinka: Nigeria's Leading Social Critic". *New York Times Review of Books,* 24 December. (1972): 6-10.

Lawrence, Margaret. "Voices of Life, Dance of Death: Wole Soyinka." *Long Drums and Canons: Nigerian Dramatists and Novelists.* London: Macmillan, (1968): 11-76.

Lindfors, Bernth. "Beating the White Man at his Own Game. Nigerian Reactions to the 1986 Nobel Prize in Literature." *Black American Literature Forum.* 22.3 (1988): 475-488.

Menon, Ritu. "The Age of Innocence." *Women's Review of Books* 14.12 September 1997. 12-15.

Mathur, O.P. "A Metaphor of Reality: A Study of the Protagonist of *Midnight's Children," Image of India in The Indian Novel in English 1960-1985.*Ed. Sudhakar Panday and R. Raja Rao.(New Delhi: Orient Longman, 1993): 113-22.

Maiti, Prasenjit. "History and Counter History: Reading Novels, reading politic: Arundhati Roy's *The God of Small Things."* May, Brian. "Back to the Future: History in/and the Postcolonial Novel." *Studies in the Novel* 23.3 (1997): 270.

Maya, D. "Woman 'Empowered'? Representation in Indian English fiction." *Samyukta* 1.2 (July 2001): 68-71.

Misra, B.L. Quest beyond Traditions: "A study of *the God Small Things*" Ed. K.A. Agarval. Indian English Fiction (2009):112-123.

Misra, Rosy. "The Crisis in Human Values in Coolie and *The God of Small Things*: A Comparative Study." Ed. Dhawan, R.K. *Indian Women Writers.* New Delhi: Prestige, (2000): 201- 209.

Mukharjee, Meenakshi. "The Anxiety of Indianess: Our Novels in English." *Mapping Cultural Spaces, Postcolonial Indian Literature in English*, Ed. by Nilufer Bharucha and Vrinda Nabar Delhi: Vision Books. (1998): 78-93.

Mendas, Ana Cristina. "Exciting Tales of Exotic Dark India: Aravind Adiga's *The White Tiger.*" *The Journal of Commonwealth Literature* 45.2. (2010): 275-93.

Mukherjee, A. Fissured skin, inner-ear radio, and a telepathic nose: The sesnses as media in Salman Rushdie's *Midnight's Children. Paragraph* 29.3 (2006):55-76.

Mijares, L. "You are an Anglo-Indian?": Eurasians and Hybridity and Cosmopolitanism in Salman Rushdie's *Midnight's Children. Journal of Common Wealth Literature.* 38.2 (2003):125-145.

Mac Dowel, Robert. "African Drama: West and South." *Africa Today* 15.4 (1968): 32-40.

Macebuh, Stanely. "Poetics and Mythic Imagination" *Critical Perspectives on Wole* Soyinka. Ed. James Gibbs. Washington D.C: Three Continents, (1980): 200-212.

Maduakor, Obiajuru. "Soyinka as a Literary Critic." *Research in African Literature* 17.1 (1986): 1-38.

Moody, David. "The Prodigal Father, Discursive Rupture in the Plays of Wole Soyinka". *Ariel* 23.1 (1992): 24-38.

Moore, Gerald. "The Uses of Myth; An examination of African Revolutionary Drama: Declarations of Cultural Independence in English Speaking World." *Ariel* 3 1 (2000): 159-70.

Moore-Gilbert, Bart. Introduction. *Postcolonial Criticism.* Ed. Bart, Moore Gilbert, Garenth Stanton, and Willy Maley. London: Longman, (1997):1-73.

Morrison, Kathleen. "To Dare Transition. Ogun as Touchstone in Wole Soyinka's *The Interpreters.*" *Research in African Literatures* 20.1 (1989): 60-71.

Mukherjee, Meenakshi. "Interrogating Postcolonialism" *Interrogating Postcolonalism: Theory, Text and context.* Ed. Harish Trivedi and Meenakshi Mukerjee, Simla: Indian Institute of Advanced Study, (1996): 3-11.

Nandi, Miriam. "Longing for the Lost (m)other- Postcolonial ambivalences in Arundhati Roy's *The God of Small Things. Journal of Postcolonial Writing.* 46.2 (2010): 175-186.

Nancy E. Batty, "The Art of Suspense: Rushdie's 1001 (Midnights)," *Ariel* 18.3 (July 1987): 94.

Narayan, Shayamala. "India" *The Journal of Commonwealth Literature* 33. (1998): 46-48.

Ogunba, Oyin. "The Traditional Content of the Plays of Wole Soyinka 1 and 2," *African Literature Today* 4 (1970): 2-18.

—.*The Movement of Transition, A Study of the Plays of Wole Soyinka.* Ibadan: Ibdan UP, 1975.

Ogungbesan, Kolawole. "Wole Soyinka and the Novelist's Responsibility in Africa." *New West African Literature* Ed. Kolawole Ogungbesan London: Heinemann, 1979: 1-8.

—."Wole Soyinka, The Past and the Visionary Writer." *A Celebration of Black and African Writing.* Ed. Bruce King and Kolawole Ogungbesan. Oxford: Oxford UP, (1977): 125-188.

Ojaide, Tanure. "Of Gods and Poets, The Ogun myth and the Poetry of Wole Soyinka". *Literary Half Yearly* XXVIII. 2 (1988): 162-171.

Oko, Akomaye. "Africa's Biggest Masquerade". *African Literature Today,* 11 (1988): 20-25.

Okoli, Tunde. "Africa's Biggest Masquerade". *Research in African Literatures.* 27.2 (1996): 94-101.

Okukwo, Juliet. "The Essential Unity of Soyinka's *The Interpreters and Seasons of Anomy.* "*African Literature Today. Myth and History.* 11 (1988): 110-121.

Olaniyan, Thejurnola. "Dramatizing Postcoloniality." *Theatre Journal* 4 (1992): 485-99.

Osofisan, Ferni. "Myth and the Revolutionary Ethics; The Humanistic Dilemma." *Journal of Commonwealth Literature* 22.1 (1987): 15-26.

—."Tiger on Stage: Wole Soyinka and Nigerian Theatre." *Theatre in Africa.* Ed. Oyin Ogunba, Abiola and Irele. Ibadan: Ibadan UP, (1978): 151-175.

—."Wole Soyinka and a Living Dramatist, a Playwright's Encounter with Soyinka's Drama." *Wole Soyinka, An*

Appraisal. Ed. Adewale Maja Pearce: London: Heinemann, (1994): 43-60.

Osundare, Niju. "Words of Iron and Sentences of Thunder'. *Research in African Literatures* 31.1 (2000): London: Heinemann, 1989: 147-155.

Prakash, Nirmala C. "*The God of Small Things*: A Tale of Mombattis." Brave Struggle. *Point of View* 5.2 (1998): 96-100.

Prakash, Gyan. "Subaltern Studies as Postcolonial Criticism." *The American Historical Review* 99.5. December, 1994.

Prasad, Amarnath. "The Cultural Milieu of Arundhati Roy's *The God of Small Things*. Pandey, Mithilesh K. Ed. *Recent Indian Novelists in English: Critical Perspectives*. New Delhi: Sarup, (2000):190-211.

Pillai, C. Gopinatha. "Aesthetics of Post colonial Feminism: A Reading of *The God of Small Things*." Eds. Jaydipsinh Dodiya, Joya Chakravarti, The critical Studies of Arundhati Roy's *The God of Small Things*. New Delhi: Atlantic Publishers and Distributors, 1999.

Prasad, Amar Nath. "Arundhati Roy's *The God of Small Things: A Novel of Psycho-Analytical Treatment*." Ed. Prasanna Sree, *Indian Women Writing in English: New Perspectives*. New Delhi: Sarup & Sons, 2005.

Peek, Andrew. "Wole Soyinka. Child of Ogun." *CRNLE* 2 (1986): 1-6.

Phelps, Gilbert. "Two Nigerian Writers: Chinua Acheba and Wole Soyinka." *The Present, The New Pelican Guide to English Literature*. Ed. Borisford. Vol. 8. Harmondsworth: Penguin, 1983: 328-343.

Ready, Richard M. "Through the Intricacies of the Fourth Stage." *Black American Literature Forum* 22.4 (1988): 711-721.

Reed, Ishmael. "Soyinka among the Mono-culturalists." *Black American Literature Forum* 22.4 (Winter 1988): 705-709.

Richard, Rene. "Self-Liberation in *A Dance of the Forests*. The Two Levels." *Commonwealth Essays and Studies* 12.2 (1990): 68-85.

Richards, David. "Proverbs like Horses. Wole Soyinka's *Death and the King's Horseman." Journal of Commonwealth Literature* XIX. 1 (1986): 86-97.

Rushdie, Salman. "Reclaiming a City and a History." *Express Magazine,* March 11, 1984: 5.

Rama Rao, Vimla, J., Sindhu N., Nirmala C. Prakash. "Arundhati Roy's" *The God of Small Things:* A Spectrum Response. *The Journal of Indian Writing in English* 2 26 (July 1998): 28.

Rangini, Ramachandra. "*The White Tiger:* Yet Another Book Fiasco?" *The Journal of Indian Writing in English* 37.1 (Jan 2009):1-10.

Saini, Bimalji. "*The God of Small Things*-A Feminist Analysis." Ed. Manmohan K. Bhanatagar, *Feminist English Literature.* New Delhi: Atlantic Publishers and Distributors, 1999.

Schultheis, Alexandra W. "Post-colonial lack and Aesthetic promise in *The Moor's Last Sigh. Twentieth century Literature* 47.4 (2001): 569-96.

Slemon, Stephen. "Post–Colonial Allegory and the transformation of History," *The Journal of Common Wealth Literature* 23.1 (1988):160.

Sawhney, Hirsh. "India: A View from Below Aravind Adiga with Hirsh Sawhney." *The Times Literary Supplement* 22 (Sept. 2006):5-16.

Syed, Mujeebuddin. "*Midnight's Children* and Its Indian Con-Texts." *Journal of Common Wealth Literature* XXIX.1 (1994):95-108.

Singh, Alka. "Arundhathi Roy: Woman as a Writer with reference to *The God of Small Things.*" *The Common Wealth Review* Xviii.2 (2009): 122-128.

Sebastian, A.J. "Poor-Rich Divide in Aravind Adiga's *The White Tiger.*" *Journal of Alternative Perspective in the Social Sciences* 1.2 (2009): 229-245.

Singh, Alka. "Arundhathi Roy: Woman as a Writer with reference to *The God of Small Things.*" *The Common Wealth Review* Xviii.2 (2009): 122-128.

Shameem, A. "Post-colonial intervention of cultural Hybridity of the Diaspora as portrayed in Kiran Desai's *The Inheritance of Loss. The Journal of Indian Writing in English* 35.2 (July 2007): 49-53.

Slemon, Stephen. "Magic Realism as Post-Colonial Discourse." *Canadian Literature* 116 (1988): 9-24.

Srivastava, N. "Languages of the nation in Salman Rushdie's *Midnight's Children* and Vikram Seth's *A Suitable Boy.*" *Ariel* 36.2 (2005): 207-231.

Sadak, S. "Colour Play in Arundhati Roy's *The God of Small Things*." Ariel 39.7 (2008): 73-84.

Sabor, Peter. "Wole Soyinka and the Scribberians." *World Literature Written in English* 29.1 (1989): 43-52.

Slemon, Stephen. "Monuments of Empire: Allegory / Counter-Discourse /Post-colonial Writing." *Kunapipi* 9.3 (1 987): 1-16.

Soyinka, Wole. "Live Burial." *A Shuttle in the Crypt.* Methuen: London, 1972.

—. "Actuality, Political Engagement, Literature, Change: An Interview with Wole Soyinka." By Jeffrey A Portnoy. *WLWE* 32-33: 2-1 (1992-93): 1-11.

—. "A Fate Worse Than Imperialism." Interview NPQ, Summer 2000: 58-59.

—. "A Transition Interview." By Biodun Jeyifo. *Transition* (1973): 62-64.

—. "An Evening with Wole Soyinka." Interview with Antony Appiah. *Black American Literature Forum* 22.4 (1988): 777-785.

—. "An interview with Wole Soyinka." By Henry Louis Gates. Black *World* 24.10 (1975): 30-48.

—. "Wole Soyinka: Individualism Vs Social Commitment". *Littcrit* 18.1(1992): 71-79.

—. "Contemporary Authors." Interview New Revision Series, Vol. 82. Dateline 25 February. 2004.

—. "I met Obickwa after war began" *Daily Times.* Nigeria, 13 Oct. 1969: 2-8.

—. "Interview with Wole Soyinka." An Interview by John A. Stotesbury. *Kunapipi* IX. 1 (1987): 55-64.

—. "Posting in Usenet Group." Online Posting Soc. Culture. Nigeria 27 March, 1997. 20 March 200 1 <SOCc. ulture.nigeria>

—. "Postmortem for a Death. An Interview by Laura Jones and Henry Gates Jr." *Black American Literature Forum* 22.4 (1988): 787-803.

—. "Soyinka in Zimbabwe. A Question and Answer Session". *Literary Half Yearly* XXVIII.2 (1987): 50-110.

—. "Talking with African Writers. Interviews with African Poets, Playwrights and Novelists" An Interview by Jane Wilkenson. London: Heinemann, 1992.

—. "Towards a Sustainable Vision of Nigeria." A Text of Speech, Internet, Date line 3 1-7-2001. Time 1 :30.

—. "Twice Bitten: The Fate of Africa's Culture Producers". PMLA 105.1 (1990): 110-120.

—. "When the Man Died: Views, Reviews and Interview on Wole Soyinka's Controversial Book". By John Agetua. Dateline 23-3-200 1, (1-12).

—. "Writing, Theater, Arts and Political Activism. Conversation with Nobel Laureate Wole Soyinka." Interview by Hw~yK reisler. Institute of International Studies. UC Berkley, 16 April 1998. 1-7.

—. "Wole Soyinka". Interview by Nathan Gardels *Progressive* 6 1.8 (1997): 36-39.

—.Interview. "Not mine, Nor yours, Only ours." *Nigerians in America.* 7 July 2001, 1-10.

—.Introduction *The Bachae of Euripedes.* By Soyinka. London: Heineinann, 1973.

—."Why I am a Secular Humanist." Interview with Norm R. Allen Jr. *Free Inquiry Magazine 17.4.* Date line 18-6-2004.

Spivak, Gayathri Chakravarthy. *In Other worlds: Essays in Cultural Politics* London: Methuen, 1987.

Thwaites, Tony. "More Tramps at Home: Seeing Australia First." *Meanjin* 46.3 (1987): 400-9.

Ten Kortenaar, Neil. "*Midnight's Children* and the Allegory of History." *Ariel* 26.2 (1995):41-62.

Trousdale, Rachel. "City of Mongrel Joy": Bombay and the Shiv Sena in *Midnight's Children* and *The Moor's Last Sigh.*" *Journal of Common Wealth Literature* 39.2 (2004):95-110.

Tickell, Alex. "*The God of Small Things:* Arundhati Roy's Postcolonial Cosmopolitanism." *Journal of Common Wealth Literature* 38.1 (2003): 73-89.

Tiffm, Helen, "Post-colonial Literatures and Counter-Discourse." _Ku-naPpl i 9.3 (1987): 17-34.

—.Introduction *Past the Last post: Theorising post-colonialism and post-Modernism.* Ed. Ian Adam and Helen Tiffm. Hampstead: Wheatsheaf, 1991: VII-XV.

Trivedi, Harish. "India and Postcolonial Discourse." *Interrogating Postcolonialism: Theory, Text and Context.* Ed. Harish Trivedi and Meenakshi Mukherjee. Shimla: Indian Institute of Advanced Study, 1996: 231-247.

Veena, Shukla. "Untouchability and Social Exclusion in Arundhati Roy's *The God of Small Things. Journal of Alternative Perspectives in the Social Sciences* 1.3(2009): 963-967.

Vijayasree: C. "Writing Off The Nations: On Notions of Nation." *Postcoloniality Reading Literature.* Ed. C.T. Indira and Meenakshi Shivram Delhi: Vikas, 2000: 33-43.

Viswanathan, Gowri. "Currying Favor: The Politics of British Educational and Cultural Policy in India, 1813-1854." *Social Text* 19-20 (1988): 85-104.

Walder, Dennis. *Postcolonial Literatures in English: History, Language, Theory.* London: Blackwell, 1999.

Watson, Ivan. "Denouncing Dictators." *Newsweek,* 10 Aug. 200 1. Dateline 15- 1-2004.

Weales, Gerald. "Wole Soyinka: Yoruba plays for all Tribes". *The Hollins Critic* XI.5 (December 1974): 1-15.

Williams, Adebayo. "Ritual and the Political Unconscious." *Research in African Literatures* 24.1 (1 993): 67-79.

Wilson H.W. ed. *Nobel Prize Winners.* London: Methuen. 1997.

Wright, Derek. "Pre- and Post-modernity in Recent West African Fiction" *Commonwealth Essays and Studies. Interspaces* 21.2 (1999): 5-17.

—. "Ritual and Revolution in Soyinka's Dramatic Theory." *Ariel* 23.1 (Jan 1992): 39-57.

—. "Transition and Grotesque: Soyinka's *Madmen and Specialists*" *Common Wealth, The Post-colonial Imagination* 18.2 (1996): 21-26.

Wright, Rob. "The Human Voice. Wole Soyinka Speaking to World Bank audience". September 1999. Dateline 21 Jan. 1994.

Wilson, Keith. "*Midnight's Children* and Reader Responsibility." *Central Quarterly* 26.3 (Autumn, 1984): 23.

West, Frank, and Westie, Margaret L. "The Social–Distance Pyramid: Relationships Between caste and class." *The American Journal of Sociology* 73.2 (Sep.1997): 67-78.

Yankowitz, Susan. "The Plays of Wole Soyinka." *Africans Forum* 1.4 (1996): 129-33.

Young, Robert J. *Postcolonialism: An Historical Introduction.* London: Blackwell, 2000.

—.*Colonial Desire. Hybridity in Theory, Culture and Race.* London: Routledge, 1994.

Zell, Hans, and Hell Silver, ed. *A Reader's Guide to African Literature.* London: Heinemann, 1972.

Zubrezycki, John. "Lower castes still stuck on India's Bottom Rung." *The Christian Science Monitor* 89.193 29 (August. 1997): 26-32.

IV. Films

Aakrosh. Dir. Priyadarshan. Perf. Ajay Devgan, Akshay Khanna and Bipasha Basu. Tirru, 2011. Film.

Ankur. Dir. Shayam Benegal. Perf. Shabana Azmi, Anat Nag, Sadhu Meher and Priya Tendulkar. Blaze, 2001. Film.

Earth. Dr Deepa Mehta. Perf. Aamir Khan, Maia Sethna, Nandita Das and Shabana Azmi. Giles Nuttgens, 1998. Film.

Gandhi. Dir. Richard Eden Borough. Perf. BenKingsley. Colombia Pictures, 1982. Film.

Gandhi, My Father. Dir. Feroz Abbas Khan. Perf. Akshay Khanna, Darshan Jariwala and Shefali Shetty. David Mc Donald, 2007. Film.

Pinjar. Dir. Chandraprakash Dwidedi. Perf. Umila Matondkar, Manoj Bajpai. Santosh Thundiyil, 2003. Film.

Shatranj Ke Khilari. Dir. Satya Jith Ray. Perf. Sanjeev Kumar, - Mirza Sajjad Ali, Saeed Jaffrey and Mir Roshan Ali. Deviki Chitra, 1997. Film.

V. Interviews

Midnight's Children Events: "Interview with Salman Rushdie & President Lee Bollinger." Colombia University. March 22, 2003. *You Tube.* Web.6 Jan 2012.

Midnight's Children's events: "From Novel to Dramatic presentation." Colombia University. March 22, 2003. *You Tube.* Web. 6 Jan 2012.

Salman Rushdie on His Creative process. Emory University. April 16, 2009. *You Tube.* Web. 6 Jan 2012.

Salman Rushdie on Teaching the Novel and Reading for Pleasure. Emory University. April 16, 2009. *You Tube.* Web. 6 Jan 2012.

A Conversation with Salman Rushdie. Penny State Broadcasting Channel. March 10 2008. *You Tube.* Web 6 Jan 2012.

Salman Rushdie Interviews Tishani Doshi. Booklyn Book festival 2010. Sep 13 2010. *You Tube.* Web 6 Jan 2012.

Salman Rushdie: Indian Society and Partition. Forum channel t.v. Sep. 4.2010. *You Tube.* Web 6 Jan 2012.

Salman Rushdie June 18, 2008. In Conversation With Michael Krasny. San Fransico, CA Courtesy of City Arts and Lectures. 5 July 2008. *You Tube.* Web. 6 Jan 2012.

Chai Time Live in Studio- Part 1 and 2- Kiran Desai, Booker Prize winning author. July 30 2009. *You Tube.* Web. 5 Jan. 2012.

Arundhati Roy discusses The God of Small Things on Book Club. Roy groupies. October 4. 2011 courtesy by BBC Radio Book club. *YouTube.* Web. 5 Jan. 2012.

Chomsky-Roy Q and A 1 of 2. MIT 2010. *You Tube.* Web. 5 Jan 2012.

Chomsky-Roy Q and A 2 of 2. MIT 2010. *You Tube.* Web. 5 Jan 2012.

Arundhati Roy and David Barsamian. Seattle Town Hall August 17.2004. *You Tube.* Web 6 Jan 2012.

Arundhati Roy with Avi Lewis, 24 March 2010. You Tube. Web 5 Jan 2012.

Arundhati Roy speaks on Operation Green Hunt. Kolkata University Institute Hall 14 April 2010. *You Tube.* Web. 5 Jan. 2012.

Riz Khan- Arundhati Roy – 02 Nov 2009- Pt 2. You Tube. Web 5 Jan. 2012. *Arundhati Roy on Face-to-Face with Karan Thapar (part 1&2).* 7 July 1999. *You Tube.* Web. 5 Jan 2012.

Booker prize Winner Desai: If only Bush read Books part 1& 2. June 11 208. *You Tube.* Web. 5 Jan. 2012.

Norris, Michele. *Kiran Desai and The Inheritance of Loss.* Jan. 3 2006. *You Tube.* Web. 5 Jan 2012.

In an interview, Rushdie tells us that he is convinced of the existence of the supernatural world. 'Network East,' BBC2, Sept. 24, 1998.

Wise, Gordon. Interview with Salman Rushdie, G*entleman,* February, 1984, p. 59.

Rushdie, Salman, Interview, BBC, 2 Sept.11, 1998. 31.

...Interview. *Northern India Patrika.* 16 Jan. 1983.

Eleanor Watchel. "An Interview with Kiran Desai," *Brick,* 79 (2007):89-108.

Wachtel. "An Interview with Kiran Desai." 105-06.

Rachel Giese. "A Passage from India: An Interview with Booker Winner Kiran Desai" (Nov. 2006) Web.

Durix, Jean-Pierre. "Salman Rushdie: Interview." *Kunapipi* 4.2 (1982): 17-26. Print.

Pattayanak, Chandrabhanu. "Interview with Salman Rushdie." *Literary Criterion* 18.3 (1983): 19-22. Print.

Webliography

www.salman-rushdie.com/www.salman-rushdie.com/. Accessed on 2 Jan. 2012.

http://en.wikipedia.org/wiki/Salman_Rushdie. Accessed on 1 Jan. 2012.

http://www.nytimes.com/books/99/04/18/specials/rushdie.html. Accessed on 1 Jan. 2012.

http://books.hindustantimes.com/2012/01/salman-rushdie-to-attend-jaipur-lit-fest/>. Accessed on 3 Jan. 2015.

http://timesofindia.indiatimes.com/topic/Salman-Rushdie>. Accessed: 21 Sept. 2015.

http://www.theparisreview.org/interviews/5531/the-art-of-fiction-no-186-salman-rushdie>. Accessed on 3 Sept. 2015.

http://www.haaretz.com/weekend/magazine/interview-salman-rushdie-is-not-afraid-1.389961>. Accessed on 2 Jan. 2015.

http://voices.yahoo.com/an-exploration-identity-salman-rushdies-midnights-178002.html>. Accessed on 25 Oct. 2015.

"Ibn Sina (Avicenna)." Islamic Philosophy Online 2004 ttp:// www.muslimphilosophy.com/sina/default.htm. Accessed on 3 Jan. 2015.

http://www.foliosociety.com/book/MDC/midnights-children>. Accessed on 3 Jan. 2015.

http://www.eb.com:1801cgibin/? DocF=micro/1081/70.html>. Accessed on 1 Jan. 2015.

www.nytimes.com/2006/2/12 books/review/12mishra.html>. Accessed on 2 Jan. 2015.

http://social.class.ncsu.edu/ jouvert/v4i3/rathl.htm>. Accessed on 4 Jan. 2015.

http:/en.wikipedia.org/wiki/Black_comedy>. Accessed on 4 Jan. 2015.

Http://Www.Time.Com/Time/Magazine/Article/0, 9171, 829868, 00.Html>. Accessed on 5 Jan. 2015.

http://www.bookbrowser.com/author_interviews/full/index.cfm? authornumber=155 2. Accessed on 3 Jan. 2015.

http://www.gaurdian.co.uk/books/2008/act/16/booker-prize>. Accessed on 2 Jan. 2015.

http://Wwwanswers.Com/Topic/Carnivalesque>. Accessed on 2 January 2015.

http://Www.Progressive.Org/Intv0401.Html>. Accessed on 4 January 2015.

www.thehindu.com/opinion/lead/article2379704.ece?homepage=true. Accessed on 4 Jan. 2015.

http://www.newstatesman.com/asia/2011/07/arundhati-roy-india-book. Accessed on 4 Jan. 2015.

www.zcommunications.org/zspace/arundhatiroy. Accessed on 5 Jan. 2015.

http://www.guernicamag.com/interviews/2356/roy_2_15_11/. Accessed on 2015.

http://blogs.reuters.com/india/2010/10/28/arundhati-roy-kashmir-remarks/. Accessed on Jan. 2015.

http://www.thenewcanon.com/god_of_small_things.html. Accessed on 5 Jan. 2015.

http://bookreviews.bookrack.in/2011/05/god-of-small-things-1997-arundhati-roy.html. Accessed on 6 Jan. 2015.

http://www.postcolonialweb.org/india/roy/nishant1.html. Accessed on January 2015.

http://www.bbc.co.uk/iplayer/episode/b015brn8/Bookclub_Arundhati_Roy_The_God_of_Small_Things/. Accessed on 6 Jan. 2015.

http://www.nytimes.com/2006/02/12/books/review/12mishra.html?pagewanted=al l. Accessed on 6 Jan. 2015.

http://www.newyorker.com/reporting/2011/04/18/110418fa_fact_desai. Accessed on 6 Jan. 2015.

http://www.meettheauthor.com/bookbites/1267.html. Accessed on 6 Jan. 2015.

http://www.npr.org/templates/story/story.php? storyId=5081531. Accessed on 6 Jan. 2015.

http://www.guardian.co.uk/books/2009/nov/14/inheritance-loss-desai-book-club Accessed on January 2015.

Index